THE LIBRARY OF
PHILOSOPHY AND THEOLOGY

Edited by

JOHN MCINTYRE AND IAN T. RAMSEY

THEOLOGY AND METAPHYSICS

THEOLOGY AND METAPHYSICS

JAMES RICHMOND

SCM PRESS LTD
BLOOMSBURY STREET LONDON

334 01703 3
FIRST PUBLISHED 1970
© SCM PRESS LTD 1970
PRINTED IN GREAT BRITAIN BY
WESTERN PRINTING SERVICES LTD
BRISTOL

FOR MARGO

CONTENTS

CONTENTS

PREFACE

THERE are two main reasons for the composition of this little book. First, I should like to pursue further and develop more positively some themes developed in an earlier work,[1] themes which have appeared to me and to others to demand further treatment. Hopefully, one aspect of this development will consist of drawing together some threads to be found both in Continental theology and in Anglo-Saxon post-analytic philosophical theology, threads which some may have regarded hitherto as disparate and unrelated. That is, it is hoped that this book will bring a certain unity into some geographically unrelated types of philosophical theology. Second, I should like to add my contribution to the contemporary concentration of attention and effort upon the problem of *natural theology*. I hope to demonstrate below that the history of both recent theology and philosophy has shown that this is a problem which theologians and philosophers cannot ignore or dismiss. And with regard to the theological side of the matter, it does not seem to me implausible to maintain that there is a real danger of many theologians in the last quarter of the twentieth century pursuing their enquiries in the conviction that the group of problems which have traditionally clustered around the ancient term 'natural theology' have now finally been disposed of; and that in the future theological constructions must be attempted in isolation from any solutions which might be given to them. This book is written in the light of the thesis that any such conviction, seriously maintained and consistently put into practice, is not merely wrong but theologically suicidal.

No claim whatsoever is made here that the approach to

natural theology discussed and developed in these pages is the only or indeed the best one. Rather, I agree strongly with those who plead today for a theological pluralism. For example, Dr E. L. Mascall, after stressing the complexity of the contemporary human situation and the wide differences to be found in human temperaments and attainments, has this to say: 'In all probability, not one but a number of approaches need to be developed if Christian theism is to display its relevance and attractiveness to the wide variety of persons who together make up the human race today.'[2] And Dr John Macquarrie, after describing the theology of the mid 'sixties ('the decadence of the dilettantes') as that of the popular paperback, the *Time* magazine articled and the television interview, predicts that we are now about to enter an era when problems will be explored in real depth in substantial, detailed and often difficult theological books. And having mentioned those perennial questions which lie close to the heart of all Christian discussion, Macquarrie has this to say:

> I do not think that there will be only one way of seeking to answer these questions. Let me confess that I get turned off every time I open a book of theology and read on the first page that this is the *only* way that it can be done! Theology is likely to be pluralistic, and I don't see the possibility of either a grand synthesis or of one type supplanting all the others. Theologians will tackle the problems they consider most important, and they will use the methods which they find most fruitful. Some of the problems will be new, but there is a large unfinished agenda passed on to us; likewise, some of the methods and perspectives may be new, but there are still unexhausted resources in Biblical theology, existentialism, process theology, hermeneutical studies, phenomenology and so on.[3]

These are words of wisdom and I should like to underline my agreement with them. But although I should disown any claim to uniqueness in the approach I have outlined, I should nevertheless claim that it takes up and combines some of the most important and relevant insights and approaches in recent philosophical theology.

In other words, I should not claim much originality in the sense that the reader may not find here much new material that he would not find elsewhere, scattered, inconveniently perhaps, through a multitude of books, papers and articles. But I should

claim a certain *Wisdomian* originality; that is, although not many
radically new materials are introduced, I yet hope to have
drawn some new connections between old ones; I hope that I
may help some readers to view old materials in strikingly novel
ways, which will deepen for them the significance of much that
has been said and written in recent years.

Perhaps a word or two on the title would be helpful. The
choice of the title *Theology and Metaphysics* does not, of course,
mean that the book claims to explore with any fullness the difficult problem of the relationship between theology and metaphysical speculation (but its author hopes that it does cast a
little light on the problem). The title originated in this way. In
the last third of the nineteenth century the eminent and influential German systematic theologian Albrecht Ritschl brought out
his *Theology and Metaphysics*,[4] in which he pleaded for the
complete and final separation of modern theology from every
form of metaphysical speculation. The significance of Ritschl's
book is twofold: on the one hand, its argument presupposed the
validity of much anti-metaphysical polemic which had been in
the air since Kant; and, on the other, the plea which runs
through the book has had an incalculably large effect on subsequent Protestant theological thinking, not merely on members
of the Ritschlian school itself, but also on important twentieth-
century anti-metaphysical theologians who were educated by
members of the school early in the century, such as Karl Barth,
Rudolf Bultmann and Dietrich Bonhoeffer. The title has therefore been filched from Ritschl; but, I would add, openly and
deliberately filched. Whereas Ritschl's book was typical of and
influential upon that type of Christian thought which seeks to
be independent of all metaphysical visions and schemes, this
little book insists, to the contrary, that any satisfactory and
healthy Christian theology simply cannot dispense with, or be
constructed in isolation from, some overall metaphysical scheme
or vision which somehow articulates into a rational unity man's
experience and knowledge of the world, taken in the widest
possible sense.

If this little work helps anyone to see that this is so, and stimulates anyone to think seriously about those issues traditionally considered under the title 'natural theology', its author will be more than satisfied. In the composition of these pages, I am once more deeply indebted to my wife, not only for much practical help, but also for much patient forbearance.

University of Lancaster   James Richmond

NOTES

1. *Faith and Philosophy*, London and Philadelphia, 1966.
2. *Theology and the Future*, London, 1968, p. 58.
3. 'What's Next in Theology?', in *The Tower* (Alumni Magazine of Union Theological Seminary, New York), Spring 1969, p. 3.
4. *Theologie und Metaphysik: Zur Verständigung und Abwehr*, Bonn, 1881 and 1887.

I

THE PROBLEM OF NATURAL THEOLOGY: CONTINENTAL EUROPE

I.1 It is first necessary to enquire what is meant by 'natural theology' in this context. This is perhaps best done by a brief examination of several definitions. 'Natural theology is traditionally that knowledge about God and the divine order which man's reason can acquire without the aid of (supernatural) revelation.'[1] This definition reflects the Platonic-Stoic identity of 'natural' and 'rational'; hence, 'natural theology is rational reflection on the question of divine existence'.[2] The term may usefully be considered from the standpoint of a different definition; thus, natural theology may be defined as the term 'applied to metaphysical ontology in so far as the general doctrine of being necessarily includes some statement about the absolute being of God'.[3] The key word in this definition is 'necessarily'. The logic of the use of this word is the conviction that being as such (reality-in-general) cannot be fully or adequately described ('doctrine') without some reference in the description to the divine existence. The only possible interpretation of this is that it is being asserted that a reference to the divine existence is necessary in order that reality may somehow be *explained*. That means, that a natural (or rational) theology must in some sense make a puzzling world plain; it must be some kind of *explanatory* or *clarificatory* theory.[4] It may be helpful to consider another term which used to be considered equivalent to natural theology, namely 'metaphysical theology'.[5] Metaphysics may be taken, with R. W. Hepburn, as the construction of some science of 'being' (reality-in-general) so that we somehow penetrate beyond 'appearance' to 'reality'. Hepburn makes the further point that the aim of metaphysicians has included 'the systematic

presentation of a vision of the world as a whole'.[6] It is therefore
easy to see why many rational theologians have been sympathetic to the metaphysical enterprise: the metaphysical theologian has attempted to penetrate beyond the *appearance* of
things to their *reality* in God (as Ground); he has tried to syste-
matize a vision of the world as a whole which *necessarily* includes
the divine order.

I.2   In the light of these definitions, it is not too difficult to list
certain defining characteristics of natural theology. First, it must
be a *rational* construction: it must appeal to human reason, to
thinking and reflecting people who are puzzled by the world
around them. Second, it must have as its subject-matter the
world as a 'whole' ('being as such', 'reality-in-general'); alternatively, we might say that it must appeal to human experience
in its widest possible sense. Third, it must somehow penetrate
'beyond' appearance to reality; it must refer somehow 'beyond'
the world as this is present to the senses. Fourth, it must be
'explanatory': it must by necessity refer to the divine existence
in order to explain what would otherwise be left puzzling and
unclear: its intellectual attraction must reside in its power to
make plain what is obscure. From these characteristics we may
attempt a tentative and comprehensive definition of natural
theology: natural theology is the rational construction of a vision
of the world as a whole, penetrating beyond the realm of
appearances to that of ultimate reality, a divine order which is
the sole explanation of an experienced world which would
otherwise be left obscure, puzzling and unclear.

I.3   In the light of this definition, it may be useful at this point
to give several brief examples of (now philosophically dubious)
natural theology. When the Thomist metaphysician, by means
of the principle of causality, attempts to show that the finite
world is ultimately inexplicable unless seen as grounded in God
as the first, necessary and uncaused Cause, he is formulating a
natural theology. Or when seventeenth- and eighteenth-century
metaphysical thinkers attempted to show that the appearance of

things in general (their regularity, efficiency, harmony, inter-relatedness, etc.) is puzzling and inexplicable unless we invoke the existence of a cosmic designing intelligence whose operations are analogously similar to those of human intelligence, they were formulating a natural theology. For both of these attempts are rational, they claim to take the world as whole as their datum, they attempt to penetrate beyond appearance to reality, and claim to explain puzzling or obscure states of affairs which are resistant to explanation in other terms.

I.4 For many centuries, there existed within Christendom side by side two types of theology, which were regarded as indispensably complementary. Within the Augustinian tradition, these two were seen as rooted in general and special revelation. God was regarded as having disclosed himself *generally* to all men through the operation of that divine light which floods all human understanding as such, an operation which is most apparent in the making of aesthetic and moral judgments. God was thus conceived as knowable through his effects; through the operation of that divine light of which God is the sole source. But there was also a special revelation, not available to human rationality as such: it was regarded as consisting of truths necessary for salvation, truths imparted through the history of Israel, the life and ministry of Christ, the establishment and activities of the Christian church. Within the Thomist tradition the two types were seen as rational and revealed theology (a different distinction from that taught by Augustinianism). By reason alone (i.e. unassisted by supernatural revelation) man could attain to certain theological truths, for example, *that* God is, that God of necessity possesses certain attributes, that the human soul is immortal. But certain other truths (necessary for salvation) are beyond the scope of unassisted human reason and must therefore be disclosed to man by revelation: the doctrines of the Trinity, the Incarnation and the Atonement, of supernatural grace, of man's supernatural destiny, and others. Both Augustinians and Thomists would have been astounded at the suggestion that theology was reducible to the second of the two

types, or that the second could exist viably in isolation from or
independently of the first. Much of the history of Christian
thought concerns the complex inter-relationship between these
two types. At certain periods within the history of Christendom,
it is true that any synthesis of faith and reason came under
heavy fire from within the church: even before the end of the
thirteenth century, Aquinas's stress upon the importance of
natural (as a complement to revealed) theology was questioned
by John Duns Scotus (1265?–1308), and by the middle of the
fourteenth century Scotus's disciple William of Occam (?–1349?)
had vigorously assaulted the incorporation of natural theology
into Christian doctrine. And during the sixteenth-century
Reformation, certain of the Reformers tried hard to sever
theology from any form of metaphysical speculation (see below).
Yet, at other times in Christendom the reliance upon metaphysical theology was so heavy as to be grotesque. The classic
instance of this was during the so-called Age of Reason (c. 1600–
1780), when the main problem facing Christian theologians was
that of finding a significant location for revelation within the
metaphysical theology of the period. But in our modern and
contemporary world, a really huge crisis for Christian belief was
precipitated by the radical questioning of natural theology
carried out by thinkers during the last third of the eighteenth
century, the period of the European Enlightenment. We must
now enquire about the nature of the crisis and (in this chapter)
its effect upon subsequent European (mainly German) theology.

1.5   Ninian Smart has said that 'Natural theology is the Sick
Man of Europe'.[7] Taking 'Europe' (in this chapter) as 'Continental Europe', we must ask how this state of affairs has come
about. Within German theology (from the Enlightenment to the
present) two huge, complementary influences can be seen as
operative against natural theology: these are the critical metaphysics of Immanuel Kant and Martin Luther's understanding
of the Christian faith. Whoever would understand modern
German theology must have some grasp of these influences, their
scope and method of operation.

I.6 So far as the operation of Kantianism is concerned, it is necessary to have some grasp of Kant's view of human knowledge, its scope and limits. Kant's insistence (in *The Critique of Pure Reason*) that human knowledge is a combination of the inner organizing and shaping power of the *a priori* categories of the mind (a notion derived from European rationalism) and sense-data from without (as taught by British empiricism), led him to rule metaphysical speculation out of court as illegitimate. For in metaphysical reasoning the mind reaches out 'beyond' the realm of sense-data, of spatio-temporal experience, into the realm of we know not what, where the categories lose their power to grasp, organize and shape. Metaphysics is therefore banished to the sphere of the unknowable. Metaphysical knowledge of God is therefore out of the question, since God is traditionally held to transcend the world of sense-experience. Hence it is pointless to enquire whether mind can attain to knowledge of God as he is 'in himself', as he is independently of the spatio-temporal world. It is this insistence that lies at the heart of Kant's negative discussions of the classical metaphysical proofs of God's existence, which constituted such a significant part of traditional natural theology. But Kant's epistemology involved something else of great consequence for Continental theology. It is that we cannot know things as they are 'in themselves', as they are in isolation from the knowing subject, apart from the standpoint of human cognition. They can only be known as they are related to the knowing subject; we can only know them *in relation to* mind. In Kant's terminology, we can only know them *phenomenally*, as they are related to the world of possible or actual experience. It is not to the point here to enter into a discussion of the strength and weakness of Kant's theory of knowledge: it is very much to the point to indicate its huge effect upon nineteenth- and twentieth-century German theology. The translation of Kant's critical metaphysics into modern German theology amounts to something like this: metaphysical knowledge has been shown to be out of the question; hence the attempt to construct a metaphysical theology (of anything remotely similar to the traditional type) must be given up;

since things-in-themselves lie beyond actual or possible cognition, the attempt to say anything about God as he is *independently of* the world of possible or actual experience must also be
abandoned; since things can only be known phenomenally, *in
their relation to* the knowing subject, so too we can only know God
in and through his *phenomena*, in and through his effects, his
appearances, his relations with things other than himself,
theology must henceforward restrict itself rigidly to such knowledge.

I.7 The effects of Kantianism on German intellectual history
were not immediately apparent. Rather, they were cumulative,
and it was some decades before Kantianism worked its way
firmly into the fabric of German academic theology, until that
point was reached where Kantian epistemology operated fairly
universally as a (sometimes unacknowledged) limiting and
normative presupposition. Nevertheless, before the end of the
nineteenth century, Kant was openly and gratefully acknowledged as the philosopher of Protestantism.

I.8 There is a second normative presupposition operative
within modern German theology in the shape of Luther's understanding of Christianity. That aspect of it most significant for us
here is the epistemological implications of the Lutheran stress on
the *sola fide*. At the heart of Lutheran Christianity lies the insistence that man is only properly related to God *through faith alone*.
Negatively, this excludes being related to God through *works*.
By 'works' Luther meant, of course, moral works, works of the
Jewish law or works imposed by the mediaeval penitential
system. Basically, Luther's point was the Pauline one that man
is unable to earn his justification before God by his own ethical
efforts. Now the figure of Luther, like that of Kant, still lurks
large behind many German theological discussions as a con-
trolling and limiting influence. And, as happened in the case of
Kant's philosophy, Luther's religious thinking has undergone a
thorough reinterpretation into modern theological terminology.
The point within that reinterpretation which has epistemolo-

gical implications is a certain development (legitimate or otherwise) of Luther's conception of *works*. For modern German
theologians have widened the scope of this to include not merely
ethical but also metaphysical and historical *works*. For the former of these they have found some justification in the writings
of Luther himself. For did not Luther rage against the influence
of scholastic philosophy and the God of the 'wretched Aristotle'?
This is hardly the point to engage in research into the question
of whether Luther so interpreted is Luther rightly interpreted.
It is the point to indicate that such a widespread interpretation
of the *sola fide* in Germany has combined with the influence of
Kantianism outlined above to reinforce the German suspicion
of metaphysical theology. For to attempt a metaphysical
theology is, bluntly, to attempt to earn one's salvation before
God! A secondary aspect of Luther's religious thought bears an
uncanny resemblance to an aspect of Kantianism already
mentioned. Having dismissed the 'scholastic' notion that we can
attain rationally to knowledge of God as he is 'in himself'
(parallel to Kant's denial of the *Ding-an-sich*), Luther insisted
that we can only know God as he is related to us in the process
of salvation; we can only know God as he is *pro me, pro nobis*
(parallel to Kant's restriction of knowledge to appearances,
phenomena). This is a subsidiary but significant aspect of the
anti-metaphysical tendency of German Lutheranism.

I.9　Other factors than these two (as we shall note at a later
point) have indeed produced anti-metaphysical tendencies in
modern German theology; it is nevertheless true that these two
have been so potent that to overlook their presence and operation would be seriously to misunderstand such theology, leading
to a failure to perceive why much German thought is irrelevant
to the construction of a new style of natural theology. In order
to perceive this it is necessary to trace the anti-metaphysical
tendencies in some recent representative German thinkers in a
little detail, a task which now awaits us.

I.10　For example, if we turn to the highly influential thought
of Friedrich Schleiermacher, we find there the strong insistence

that we can only know God in and through those effects (especially 'the feeling of absolute dependence') which he (in and through the pressure exerted on us by the world) generates in and evokes from us. Apart from this, insists Schleiermacher in his *Speeches on Religion,* apart from this experience, there is and can be no genuine knowledge of God. In the same work, Schleiermacher insists upon the sharp separation of religion from metaphysics, and indeed can hardly stress too strongly that genuine religion does not and cannot originate in the human *impulse to know* (i.e. in the metaphysical quest). Schleiermacher is commonly and not incorrectly classified as an immanentist theologian: for him, God is immanent within man's environment and exerts pressure upon religious subjects in and through the pressure of the world; of course, Schleiermacher *does not deny* God's independent being apart from the world of religious experience; but he *does* deny that we can have any significant knowledge of this and that it has any relevance or interest for genuine Christian theology. Despite Schleiermacher's considerable contribution to Western philosophical theology, it is perfectly fair to describe him a strongly anti-metaphysical theologian. Schleiermacher knew his Kant, knew him only too well. And although he fervently believed that he was reacting against and overcoming the limitations implicit within the work of Kant, his own Kantianism is only too apparent. He warmly welcomed the Kantian onslaught upon metaphysics as 'abolishing reason in order to make room for faith'; the abandonment of the quest for knowledge of the 'thing-in-itself' underlies his entire approach to religion; his restriction of the knowledge of God to knowledge of effects, phenomena, appearances, was one that he never relaxed nor abandoned. Yet the price which he (and his school) paid for so easily relinquishing metaphysics was a high one. Much rubbish has been written of Schleiermacher as a 'psychological subjectivist', and much else has been written which has done less than justice to the reputation of a great theologian. Nevertheless, it can hardly be denied that neither he nor his disciples were able to discuss satisfactorily the *transcendence* of God. To be sure, Schleiermacher believed that God transcended nature, that there was 'more' to him than could be experienced in genuine piety; but to the end, he was neither able nor willing to explore what this 'more' involved. It is therefore hard to condemn Feuerbach outright for interpreting Schleiermacher as saying that God had no significant being apart from his attachment to the souls and minds of humans. If we interpret the terms aright, it is not incorrect to suggest that the price Schleiermacher and his school paid for a complacent relinquishment of metaphysical exploration was to be trapped within an immanentist subjectivism which had little or no room for transcendence. Yet, the philosopher will rightly enquire, can this do anything like justice to Christian theism, in which the notion of transcendence has always been a quite essential ingredient? Schleiermacher has his profound insights (to which we shall return later); but it is hard to deny that he has little constructive help to offer those who would dearly like to see some efforts being made towards the formulation of a new-style, contemporary natural theology. And he began a trend in Continental theology which continues to the present day.

I.11   If we turn from Schleiermacher to another, later, influential Continental thinker, Søren Kierkegaard, we find ourselves in an atmosphere not merely unsympathetic to natural theology, but implacably hostile to it. Although the paucity of clear references to it in his writings are apt to deceive us on this point, Kierkegaard was (like Kant, Hegel and Schleiermacher) a child of the Enlightenment: his discussions of metaphysical theology leave us in no doubt that he saw and appreciated the point of Kant's critique of metaphysical theism. In point of fact, Kierkegaard quarrelled in the first instance with contemporary Hegelian versions of natural theology. Against Hegelian theologians who emphasized the rationality of the world, the inexorability of the Hegelian dialectic and the immanence of God within mind, the continuity between reason and faith and between philosophy and theology, Kierkegaard fiercely stressed the omnipresence of irresoluble paradox in thought and experience, the necessity of involved existential thinking nurtured by dread and suffering, the discontinuities between man and God, church and world, faith and reason, Christian and non-Christian, the utter loneliness of faith, and hence the futility of all rational attempts to attain to knowledge of God. Pro-Kierkegaard apologetic has rightly warned us that it is dangerous to interpret him in isolation from his Hegelian and Lutheran matrix and that Kierkegaard interpreters must ever bear in mind that he himself regarded his work as a *one-sided corrective* ('a little pinch of spice to impart a peculiar taste to the rest') to Hegelian philosophical theology: nevertheless, it ought to be remembered that Kierkegaard is a peculiarly twentieth-century prophet (his work was not translated from the Danish into German until the last few years of the nineteenth century), and that his work has been utilized by twentieth-century thinkers in a singularly antimetaphysical direction. Kierkegaard has profound religious insights, and his many-sided thought has been widely and deeply influential in many areas of modern thought and life; yet who could deny that from him stem strong tendencies which are antipathetic to the aspirations and aims of the speculative theologian?

I.12   If we move on to another influential German theological thinker, Albrecht Ritschl, we are confronted by someone who, as we noted above, adopted as one of his ambitions the complete and final separation of Christian theology from all forms of metaphysical speculation. An avowed Kantian (whose knowledge of the master's teaching was mediated to him by Lotze), Ritschl spelled out the meaning of Kantianism for Christianity in the form of a close-knit systematic theology. On the negative side, he accepted and presupposed the Kantian critique of metaphysics and speculative theology. On the positive side, he defined religion in terms of man's struggle to overcome brute, physical nature (nature being, in Ritschl's naturalistic and materialistic age, a force impersonally hostile to man), in order that he may attain to the fulfilment of his moral and spiritual personality (Kantian). Ritschl's Kantianism and Lutheranism were fused into a singular unity. He rejected as illegitimate all theological propositions in the form of 'theoretical judgments' (Kantian), parallel to Luther's denial that we can know God 'in his essence'. All legitimate theological propositions must be in the form of 'independent value-judgments'; they must, that is, refer to the *value* which religious realities (e.g., God, Christ, grace) have for the souls of those involved in the contradiction between spirit and nature. What God is 'in himself', independently of his value for our souls, has, declared Ritschl to the end of his life, nothing to do with genuine Christian faith or theology. Here we have a translation into nineteenth-century theological jargon of Kant's insistence that we only know things in their phenomena, in the ways in which they are related to the knowing subject, and of Luther's claim that we can only know God and Christ as they are *pro me, pro nobis*. Ritschl was the founder of a German theological school whose Kantian-Lutheran aversion to metaphysics in theology was (as we shall see at a later point) mediated to the contemporary German theological scene by his pupils and by theirs. For this reason alone, Ritschl is no theological antique, of interest only to historians of theological ideas.

I.13 When we enter the twentieth century and turn our attention briefly to the immensely influential Karl Barth, we note that the earliest significant influences to which he was exposed were strongly anti-metaphysical in character. His university training was given to him by neo-Kantian Ritschlians such as Harnack, Kaftan and Herrmann. His earliest researches were prosecuted within the area of sixteenth-century Reformation theology, which is hardly (due to historical circumstances) notable for its enthusiasm for speculative theology. And his first significant work (the *Römerbrief* of 1919) strongly betrays the influence not only of the Reformers but also the fideistic side of Kierkegaard. Thereafter, the writings of Barth are characterized by an uncompromising antipathy for natural theology (*natürliche Theologie*). And it can hardly be denied that this negative aspect of Barth's work has been just as influential as the more positive side, which has been devoted to expounding the significance and content of Christian revelation.

I.14 It is important to note that in Barth's hostility to natural theology a new, and peculiarly Continental, element enters the situation, an element already present to some degree in the hostility of Kierkegaard to 'Christendom'. The immediate background of Barth's hostility is Ritschlianism. Hostile as Ritschl was to speculative metaphysics in theology, he yet held to a form of 'natural theology'. This he derived in the last analysis from the doctrine of Kant's *Critique of Practical Reason*; religion underwrites moral values and assists man in the attainment of them. The *value* of God consists of the unique assistance which he renders to man in the development of his moral personality. The moral life (or struggle) forms the basis of Ritschl's natural theology. But if God is conceived as the divine being who joins forces with man precisely at the point where his most cherished values are threatened, it is inevitable that a close continuity, a close identity of interest and purpose, between the human and the divine is established. Hence Ritschl's disciples were eventually accused of believing in a God who was 'merely man writ large', in a 'bourgeois' God, who largely reflected the ideals and aspirations of religious man. (It could be persuasively argued that such a conception was the inevitable outcome of certain immanentist emphases in much nineteenth-century Continental religious thought, of which the thought of Hegel and that of Schleiermacher were typical, and against which Kierkegaard had protested so fiercely.) Barth's original invective against natural theology was actually rooted in his understandable dislike of what he regarded as the grotesque Ritschlian overemphasis on the continuity between man and God, and its alleged political and religious consequences. The Ritschlian conception of God, Barth insisted, practically excluded essential Christian conceptions such as the judgment of God upon all human affairs, and led, in his view, to political complacency on the part of liberal churchmen. In point of fact, Barth's decisive break with Ritischlanism came when many Ritschlians not merely tolerated but also supported the war-policies of pre-1914 Imperial Germany, which Barth saw as the inevitable outcome of the insidious tendency to deify natural man, a tendency implicit within Ritschlian natural theology. But Barth broke not merely with Ritschlianism as such: there is a sense in which Barth *broke thenceforward with reason as a source of theological truth* (but not as an intellectual tool in the service of revelation). This, then, is another root of Barth's theological 'anti-rationalism', a tendency in his thought which was reinforced by his participation in the German church struggle of the early nineteen-thirties. Barth's quarrel with the 'German Christians' sprang from his understandable dislike of their 'natural theology', their theologically systematized insistence that there existed a knowledge of divine nature and purpose in German culture, history and race, a conviction which allowed them to come to terms eventually with Nazi plans for genocide, war and the acquisition of world power. In the context of the German church struggle of the period, to admit the possibility and legitimacy of a 'natural theology' was, it is arguable, to open the doors to many forms of irresponsible lunacy.

I.15 The Barthian aversion to natural theology, so influential in the West in our own day, was conceived during a relatively short, but singularly tragic and irrational period of German cultural and political history. Yet times change; and surely the contemporary Barthian fideist is not beyond the reasonable argument that irrational times generate irrational theories, that the forms of natural theology against which Barth and his colleagues reacted so fiercely were atypical nineteenth-century versions of it, and that contemporary non-German religious cultures can hardly be expected to accept without question and qualification an extreme form of fideism reached in another age in an anxiety-ridden portion of central Europe. But such considerations do not affect the *fact* that Barthianism as an impressive theological system has strongly reinforced theological anti-metaphysical tendencies already operative in the West, influencing many theologians in the direction of a fideistic and almost exclusively biblicistic theological position.

I.16 When we turn to another twentieth-century Continental thinker whose influence upon Western religious thought is judged to have been significant, Martin Buber, we find, despite the profound and suggestive contribution made by him to philosophical theology, that we are still in a strongly *anti-metaphysical* atmosphere. When Buber elucidated the two primary words of human existence (through the speaking of which man constitutes his being in two qualitatively different ways), *I-Thou* and *I-It*, it is clear that he allocated metaphysical reasoning and discourse about God to the latter of these, and thus seriously called in question the propriety of the inclusion of metaphysics in religious thinking. For, according to Buber, God is the *Thou* who can never be or become an *It*; man is only properly related to God when encountering him in the present moment as an ever-present *Thou*. Hence the only genuine knowledge of God is that self-authenticating and propositionally incommunicable awareness of him generated in the contemporary meeting with him. It follows that not only is it impious to speak of God in the third person (as if he were absent), as speculative theology tends to do, but also that if one does so, one is not speaking of the true God at all, but of an impersonal and religiously irrelevant idol. Buber's teaching has, of course, been widely utilized by Christian apologetic theologians in order to articulate what they take to be the fundamental logic of the Christian faith, but their views have been rightly and incisively criticized by analytic philosophers of religion.[8] But the point to grasp is that once again we have a Continental religious thinker who, despite the profundity of his insights and the weight of his contribution, reinforces the Continental aversion to and dismissal of metaphysical theology.

I.17 We turn now briefly to that twentieth-century Continental theologian who is probably not only the most interesting and complex, but perhaps also the most influential of his age, Rudolf Bultmann. No one would wish to detract from the immense contribution made by Bultmann to twentieth-century religious thought. Bultmann's use of existentialism to give a picture of man as an inalienably religious being, sunk in inauthentic life and grasping ineffectually for genuine life, and his re-interpretation of the New Testament in the light of this picture, have brought before an entire theological generation a wide range of urgent questions which are quite unavoidable by contemporary workers in theology. Yet again, despite the huge and valuable contribution, and despite Bultmann's not unimportant concession that there is a certain, if negative, 'natural' knowledge of God in those existential questions raised by natural man,[9] it must not be overlooked that on his own admission Bultmann is one of the most typical of Continental anti-metaphysical theologians.[10] To investigate Bultmann's anti-metaphysical tendencies is to come firmly once more up against those German influences described above, namely Lutheranism, neo-Kantianism, Ritschlianism and Barthianism. His attempt to free Christianity from all metaphysical world-views (*Weltanschauungen*), he tells us, is motivated by a desire to implement the Lutheran *sola fide*. His attempt to restrict legitimate theological propositions to *existential* (to the exclusion of *ontological*) ones reflects clearly the neo-Kantian limitation of knowledge of things to that of phenomena and relations, the Ritschlian restriction of such propositions to the area of *value-judgments* (propositions asserting the value of religious realities for human life), and the Lutheran restriction of knowledge of such realities to what is religiously significant *pro nobis*. And despite his unconcealed antipathy for certain aspects of Barthianism, he never quarrelled with Barth on the issue of distinguishing decisively and qualitatively between authentic Christian faith on the one hand and metaphysical speculation on the other.

I.18 Hopefully, enough has been said to demonstrate how contemporary German theology tends to regard the issue of natural theology. Its presuppositional limitations are such that it can hardly be expected to offer much positive and constructive help to any programme of framing a helpful natural theology for the closing decades of the twentieth century. Yet nineteenth- and twentieth-century German theology has its profound insights which cannot be ignored. And at a later point we must ask how the insights of such theology may be related to the construction

of a contemporary natural theology (chapter V below). Moreover, it is undeniable that since the Enlightenment most of the
great creative thrusts in philosophical theology have come from
Germany, and it is arguable that European Christianity therefore owes German theological thought more than it realizes.
There is truth in this; yet, while affirming this truth, it is also
arguable that the time has come to recognize that the anti-
rational limitations inherent in a wide range of German theologies are such as to force us to enquire whether they are not in
dire need of being corrected and supplemented by another and
very different approach, one that takes speculative theology
with a much greater seriousness.

I.19   German theologies of the nineteenth and twentieth centuries have largely been in their various ways responses to logical
and epistemological challenges produced by the Enlightenment.
On the whole, it is not unfair to attempt a generalization, and to
say that they have tended to respond in one of two opposed
ways, and that each of these ways turns out to be, on analysis,
extremely problematic, and raises most sharply the question of
the need for speculative theology as a supplement and corrective. The first of these ways, typified by the approaches of
Schleiermacher, Ritschl and Bultmann, appears to limit the
data of theology strictly to *what can be experienced* (in each case
differently conceived), and affirms that what lies supposedly
beyond experience cannot be of concern or interest to genuine
theology. The second of them, typified by the approaches of one
side of Kierkegaard and the Barthian school, affirms that the
data of theology are given to man in and through a *supra-rational
revelation* which comes entirely from beyond the world and our
everyday experience, which can only be received in humility
and obedience, and which lies beyond rational analysis and
criticism. Each of these approaches, if taken on its own, appears
to lead us into the most acute and insoluble difficulties.

I.20   The main, and overwhelming difficulty (apparent to anyone who has examined German theology from Schleiermacher

to Bultmann) which attaches to the first way concerns, bluntly, the danger of transforming theology into religious anthropology. For theologians of this approach, at the end of the day, tend to be left with a collection of human data, however interesting and edifying, since on their own explicit and unambiguous admission they are not and cannot be concerned with what supposedly lies 'beyond' this data (II.20). R. W. Hepburn has made the point neatly: 'If this metaphysical task (i.e. that of delineating the transcendent) is altogether rejected by the theologian, the only account of Christianity that is still open to him is an account in terms of a pattern of human living, here and now. . . . Theology becomes "anthropology".'[11] But the grave difficulty here is that such an approach is quite unable to do justice to Christianity *in as much as* Christianity is still held to be a religion having to do essentially with a God who transcends the finite world and our experience of it, in the sense that he is the eternal cause and ground of the world. The price which these theologians have to pay for their complete rejection of metaphysics is a high one.

I.21 When we turn to the second of the two ways, appealing to a completely supra-rational revelation, the difficulties are no less severe. If the revelation appealed to is really supra-rational, it seems impossible for the defender of this view to evade the accusation that he is appealing to an entirely *arbitrary* revelation. Hence Frederick Ferré, having discussed the revelationist's rejection of rational criteria applicable to revelation, argues that only by applying such criteria '. . . could the floodgates be closed against the endless absurdities of innumerable fanatics and the weird lunacies of the deranged or the irresponsible'.[12] Ferré further quotes from H. J. Paton: 'To declare war upon reason is to alienate all who care for truth and to hold open the door for the impostor and the zealot.'[13] Paton further declares: 'Complete scepticism is a poor support, and a dangerous ally, for religion.'[14] Or we may consider some wise words from Hepburn: 'The theologian is obliged not only to expound the content of revelation, but also to justify his claim that the

revelation is from and about *God*.'[15] Or we may consider these
words from William Temple: 'To deny that revelation can, and
in the long run must, on pain of becoming manifest as supersti-
tion, vindicate its claim by satisfying reason and conscience, is
fanatical.'[16] The cumulative effect of such words should be to
remind us that there is not merely revelation but *revelations*, a fact
which forces us to compare and discriminate between them, so
involving us in the area of metaphysical theology. John Macquarrie has remarked that those theologians who welcome the
breakdown of older ways of doing natural theology and who try
to persuade us that we may make do with revealed theology
alone are '. . . left with a revelation which . . . is left suspended
in mid air, so to speak, as an arbitrary and isolated phenomenon'.[17] Nor will it at all do to assert that revelation is somehow
self-authenticating, in the sense that it contains within itself the
guarantee of its own truth! For quite apart from the logical
difficulties in the way of defining *self-authenticating*, there remains
the fact that claims to competing and mutually incompatible
revelations are invariably accompanied by claims to *self-authentication*, a fact which inserts us firmly back into the area of
rational discrimination and judgment, and hence some kind of
rational theology. The price which revelationists have to pay
for *their* rejection of metaphysics is also a high one.

I.22 We turn now to another objection to natural theology
which must be dealt with. There lingers in the minds of many
religious believers the unexamined suspicion that somehow the
claim of the metaphysical theologian that we must have criteria
applicable to revelation is an impious or even a blasphemous
one, in the sense that he appears to wish to sit in judgment upon
Almighty God. But this suspicion is based on a not uncommon
confusion of thought, best described in this way. The revelationist indeed often speaks of revelation as though it consisted of
the unambiguous, empirical, face-to-face descent of the Ancient
of Days in glory indescribable, confronting fallen and sinful man
with his judgment, grace and demand, a descent at the conclusion of which there is an insolent metaphysician insisting

upon credentials. It would be not only an impious but a brave man who would behave thus! But in point of fact the situation is quite otherwise. Revelation, unless it is an utterly solipsistic concept, is something that can only be communicated and discussed in spatio-temporal and historical symbols, words, images and propositions. If so, its vehicles are subject to finite limitations and distortions, and so cannot evade rational analysis, criticism and discrimination. There is therefore justification for the sharp words of Macquarrie: '. . . whenever any person or institution or sacred book prefaces its utterances with the formula "Thus saith the Lord", we have immediately to ask whether this expression may not be a veiled but impressive way of saying, "I'm telling you". We can only do this by testing the alleged revelation by the light of that human wisdom and philosophy which is despised by some of our theologians.'[18] We are brought again sharply to the inescapability of metaphysical theology. What is being argued here is not that 'revelation' is a vacuous or outmoded concept, but that the revealed basis of theology is just as much a *problem* for theologians as its rational basis. It only multiplies confusions if this is not recognized.

I.23 These considerations bring another point before our attention. The way of talking of the revelationist often conveys the impression that 'revelation' is an unambiguous, hard, clearly delimited datum which can be taken for granted by all concerned. But if what is said above holds true, it is quite otherwise. For many kinds of mutually incompatible things are sometimes claimed by Christians as having been *revealed*. It is notorious, for example, that in the past a section of the South African Dutch Reformed Church claimed that the theological basis for *apartheid* is revealed in the Old Testament Scriptures, and thus attempted to justify theologically the South African political and social *status quo*. Now Christians who find this claim distasteful and intolerable dispute its revealed basis on the grounds that *such a thing could not possibly have been revealed by God* (certain passages of the Scriptures notwithstanding), because it is morally offensive. A dispute of this kind reveals once more the necessity for criteria, not in this case logical or epistemological, but ethical. Once more the tasks of metaphysical theology are found to be inescapable; as the classical theologians of antiquity insisted, that which claims to be revelation must win the allegiance of both reason and conscience.

I.24 In this chapter we have noted how the basis of classical Western natural theology began to be eroded away during the European Enlightenment. We have noted briefly some of the dominant non-metaphysical responses to the Enlightenment, responses pregnant with great insight and value. Yet, the inherent limitations of German theology have been such as to prevent the question of the restoration of metaphysical theology from being taken with any great seriousness. But, paradoxically, these very limitations have helped to shape theological systems which desperately need natural theology, both as a corrective and a supplement. It is now time to turn to Anglo-Saxon circles, to enquire how natural theology has fared there.

NOTES

1. See *A Dictionary of Christian Theology*, ed. Alan Richardson, London, 1969, p. 226.

2. *Ibid.*

3. *Concise Theological Dictionary*, ed. Karl Rahner and Herbert Vorgrimler, London and Freiburg, 1965, p. 307.

4. For this aspect of natural theology, see G. F. Woods, *Theological Explanation*, London, 1958.

5. See R. W. Hepburn's article on 'Metaphysics', in *A Dictionary of Christian Theology*, pp. 212–13.

6. *Op. cit.*, p. 212.

7. In 'Revelation, Reason and Religions', *Prospect for Metaphysics*, ed. Ian Ramsey, London, 1961, p. 80.

8. See Ronald W. Hepburn, *Christianity and Paradox*, London, 1958, pp. 24–59; Frederick Ferré, *Language, Logic and God*, London, 1962, pp. 94–104.

9. See Bultmann's 'The Question of Natural Revelation' (1941), in *Essays Philosophical and Theological*, London, 1955, pp. 90–118.

10. See Bultmann's recently translated essay, 'What does it mean to speak of God?', in R. Bultmann, *Faith and Understanding*, London, 1969, pp. 53–65.

11. Art. 'Metaphysics', *A Dictionary of Christian Theology*, p. 213.

12. *Language, Logic and God*, p. 92.

13. *Op. cit.*, p. 92; from H. J. Paton, *The Modern Predicament*, London, 1955, p. 58.

14. Paton, *op. cit.*, p. 58.

15. *A Dictionary of Christian Theology*, p. 213.

16. *Nature, Man and God*, London, 1934, p. 396.

17. *Principles of Christian Theology*, London, 1966, p. 47.

18. *Twentieth-Century Religious Thought*, London, 1963, p. 334.

II

THE PROBLEM OF NATURAL THEOLOGY:
ANGLO-SAXON CIRCLES

II.1 When we turn to British circles, we note first that the beginnings of the erosion of classical natural theology may be dated, as we dated the beginnings of the same process in Continental Europe, from about the third quarter of the eighteenth century. When we enquire about the reasons for this, we come solidly up against two related factors, namely, the progress of the post-Renaissance natural sciences and the development of modern philosophical empiricism.

II.2 The significance of the first of these is to be sought in a tendency which had been operative in scientific thinking from before the end of the sixteenth century, the tendency towards *understanding and explaining the world in terms of those forces, factors and processes which are immanent within the world*; that is, without appeal or references to essences, powers or beings allegedly 'outside' or 'beyond' the spatio-temporal world. As a matter of history, this meant that in attempts to understand or explain appeals were less frequently made to *substance* (as a kind of omnipresent, invisible substratum of the physical world), to *causality* (as a universal, necessary cosmic principle), and to *God* (as a being whose activities could be invoked in order to bridge gaps in scientific understanding). We may regard this trend in modern Western scientific thinking as one significant aspect of what is nowadays fashionably called *secularization*. This is a term describing that necessary and neutral process whereby stress is laid on *this present world* (its structure and inter-relatedness) rather than on any world which supposedly lies 'beyond' or 'behind' this one. Hence, secularization in science means the attempt to understand this world in intra-mundane terms.[1]

II.3 The development of philosophical empiricism is a process which occurred almost wholly in Britain. Empiricism (as its name indicates) is an epistemological standpoint which places a heavy emphasis on *experience*. However, the development of British empiricism through Locke, Berkeley and Hume down to recent decades has meant the gradual narrowing down of experience to *sense-experience*. Hence British empiricists from Hume to the present have tended to take experience as meaning observations, perceptions, predictions based upon testable hypotheses, and the like. It is a defensible generalization that modern British philosophy developed within a society where science (with its precision-languages and veridical procedures) was greatly admired, and hence it is arguable that the development of modern empiricism is unintelligible apart from the scientific character of the society in which it was produced (II.2).

II.4 Just as the key-figure in the criticism of natural theology in Continental circles was Kant, the key-figure in Anglo-Saxon circles was David Hume. Basically Hume's contention was that genuine knowledge was expressible only by two types of statement, logico-mathematical ones and those based upon sense-impressions. Logico-mathematical expressions are significant in so far as they properly set forth the correct relations between ideas, symbols and concepts. Examples of such are mathematical equations, tautologies and definitions. But expressions which refer to the external (as contrasted with the internal, intramental) world must, Hume insisted, be ultimately referrable to experience understood as perception and observation. Claims to knowledge other than these were ruled out of court as illegitimate.

II.5 In the light of his basic ideas Hume carried out a fierce assault on metaphysics; he declared that those concepts and notions over which metaphysicians were apt to wrangle (such as 'substance', 'self', 'ultimate reality', 'mind' and, as we shall see, 'God') were pointless and that the wrangles themselves were inherently frustrating and wastefully time-consuming. This is so precisely because observations, perceptions and empirical tests which could bring the wrangles to any kind of satisfactory conclusion are inconceivable. This led Hume to regard with the utmost scepticism all assertions which referred to substances, entities and factors *outside*, *beyond* or *underlying* the spatio-temporal world which is present to the senses.

II.6 Hume's examination and rejection of natural theology, to be found mainly but not wholly in his *Dialogues Concerning Natural Religion*, is a corollary of his rejection of metaphysics. The formal topic of the *Dialogues* is the argument from design, but points made by Hume in his discussion of this have relevance far beyond the scope of this one argument. The seventeenth- and eighteenth-century form of the teleological proof made much of recent and contemporary advances in the natural sciences, especially in biology. Beginning from premises derived from these (the regularity, harmony, beauty and efficiency of the natural world), it moved, by analogy, to the existence of an intelligent designer of the cosmos to account for them. There exists no more searching examination of this argument than that found in the *Dialogues*. One point made by Hume links up with what we said of *secularization* in II.2. The theistic approach of the teleological argument may come into conflict with science. In *Dialogues* VIII Hume argues that the theistic approach arbitrarily rules out of court other potentially fruitful approaches, for example, that of materialistic atomism (Epicurean in origin, but advanced by French materialists who were contemporaries of Hume). Of course, the attitude being pleaded for by Hume is scepticism about any *metaphysical* (*i.e. non-scientific*) *approach whatsoever*. Metaphysical speculation might furnish a hundred views all mutually incompatible, and, insists Hume, the odds are 'a thousand, a million to one' if one or other of these views be the true one.[2] For Hume, the fact that the argument from design (like all other metaphysical arguments) is so radically *non-*

experimental is sufficient to warrant its dismissal by serious-minded people. This is most important; for it exhibits in Hume a distinction which lies at the heart of all positivism and empiricism, that between science and metaphysics, to which we shall return frequently. Metaphysical views cannot be empirically checked up on, scientific ones can. Metaphysical activity is therefore infinitely and intolerably time-wasting, scientific activity is not. The first should be discouraged and abandoned; the second should be encouraged and energetically pursued.

II.7 Other points made by Hume in the *Dialogues* are of considerable significance. So far as *observation* is concerned, is not the argument from design intolerably one-sided? For instance, does it not regard the world *one-sidedly* as a huge mechanical structure (thus allowing the inference by analogy to the existence of a cosmic mechanic), rather than as a huge, vegetative, self-reproducing organism, a premise not favourable to theistic reasoning?[3] Once again Hume's aim is to generate scepticism about all forms of metaphysical explanation, on the grounds that they leave the sphere of observations and veridical procedures so far behind as to relinquish all hope of ever reaching satisfactory conclusions. The point Hume is getting at once more is the radically *non-experimental* character of metaphysics. The one-sidedness of the argument is again underlined by Hume when he tries to exhibit how highly selective its defenders are in choosing their evidence; the argument can only proceed by focusing attention upon regularity, harmony, beauty and efficiency. But what, asks Hume, of disharmony, irregularity, ugliness, pain, inefficiency, waste, and so on?[4] The evidence afforded by the natural world is highly ambiguous, and the nature of the ambiguity is such that it cannot be resolved by appeal to perceptions and observations. We are once more in danger of frustrating ourselves, pointlessly consuming our time, and wastefully dissipating our energies.

II.8 The distinction which Hume wishes to draw between metaphysics on the one hand and science on the other comes out strongly in the celebrated passage with which he concludes his *Enquiry Concerning Human Understanding*.

> When we run over libraries, persuaded by these principles, what havoc must we make? If we take in our hand any volume; of divinity or school metaphysics, for instance; let us ask, *Does it contain any abstract reasoning concerning quantity or number?* No. *Does it contain any experimental reasoning concerning matter of fact and existence?* No. Commit it then to the flames: for it can contain nothing but sophistry and illusion.[5]

One must note carefully here Hume's preference for logico-mathematical and experimentally-testable reasoning over against (experimentally-untestable) metaphysical reasoning, a distinction crucial for our understanding below of twentieth-century positivism and empiricism.

II.9   Hume's treatment of causal arguments for God's existence is not essentially dissimilar. For when it is argued (as it commonly is) that state of affairs *B* in the spatio-temporal world *must have been caused* by state of affairs *A* in the same world, there is in principle a way of checking the argument. This is by the observation of *sequences* where *B*s have occurred and by enquiring about the observable antecedent occurrence of *A*s within the sequences. To be sure, in Hume's view the element of necessity ('must have been caused') is a wholly subjective one, based upon a habit of mind (the habituation of mind to *B*s being preceded by *A*s); nevertheless, Hume insisted upon the soundness of the argument in that it is based upon an experimentally testable 'natural belief'. But with theistic causal arguments the case is quite otherwise. The universe is a quite *unique* 'state of affairs';[6] so therefore must its cause be. There are no perceptible sequences of events in which universes occur which would allow the observer to reach either *statistically probable* conclusions or 'natural beliefs' about the activities of causal deities within the sequences. Yet once more, the attractiveness of metaphysical explanations lures us into an infinitely time-consuming and energy-dissipating area where experimental testing and checking are out of the question.

II.10   There is one further aspect of Hume's dismissal of metaphysics which we must mention, not only for its intrinsic importance but also for the significance which it has for our discussion in a later chapter (VI). As a radical and consistent empiricist there was one much discussed aspect of reality with which Hume could not fail to deal, namely, human personalities. The question of the *self*, as we shall argue later, has always been a tricky one for empiricists. When people (people in general, not only Cartesian dualists) use language referring to 'souls' or 'selves' it is clear that they mean something that exists 'in reality'. In Humean terminology, they are referring to a 'matter of fact and existence'. Yet clearly a *self* is not something that is *observable* in anything like Hume's sense, and it is not easy to conceive of how *selves* could become the subject of 'experimental reasoning' in anything like the way intended by Hume. If Hume was to be radical and consistent in his empiricism, he was clearly obliged completely to deny us knowledge of an unobservable, non-spatio-temporal, enduring reality referred to by much ordinary language about the self. This is precisely what he did.[7] Hume pleaded strongly for utter scepticism with regard to the traditional metaphysical enquiry about the nature of that imperceptible 'substance' in which perceptions and thoughts are supposed to 'inhere', on the grounds of the extreme obscurity of any notion we may reach about such a 'substance'. The nature of the substance and the nature of the alleged *inhesion* are equally incomprehensible. Hume therefore asks: 'What possibility then of answering the question, *Whether perceptions inhere in a material or immaterial substance*, when we do not so much as understand the meaning of the question?'[8] Indeed, he regards the obscurity as so huge as to reject *all* metaphysical accounts of the soul, including those of idealistic dualists and materialists.[9] When we consider human personality, of what will Hume allow us knowledge? His answer is that our knowledge must be strictly limited to that of *perceptions*. The crucial passage of the *Treatise* is worth quoting in full:

> I may venture to affirm of . . . mankind, that they are nothing but a bundle or collection of different perceptions, which succeed each other with an inconceivable rapidity, and are in a perpetual flux and movement. Our eyes cannot turn in their sockets without varying our perceptions. Our

thought is still more variable than our sight; and all our other senses and faculties contribute to this change; nor is there any single power of the soul, which remains unalterably the same, perhaps for one moment. The mind is a kind of theatre, where several perceptions successively make their appearance; pass, repass, glide away, and mingle in an infinite variety of postures and situations. There is properly no *simplicity* in it at one time, nor *identity* in different, whatever natural propension we may have to imagine that simplicity and identity. The comparison of the theatre must not mislead us. They are the successive perceptions only, that constitute the mind; nor have we the most distant notion of the place where these scenes are represented, or of the materials of which it is composed.[10]

This, then, is a statement of Hume's celebrated 'bundle' theory of the self. We must note carefully that Hume is not asserting that the soul does not exist; he is arguing that this proposition (and its denial) lie outside the scope of knowledge and discussion, because they lie outside the scope of *observation*.[11] '. . . When I enter most intimately into what I call *myself*, I always stumble on some particular perception or other . . . I can never catch *myself* at any time without a perception, and can never observe anything but the perception.'[12] Hume's treatment of our knowledge of the self is completely parallel to his treatment of our knowledge of God; discussions and enquiries about the existence of the one are as time-consuming and energy-dissipating as those about the existence of the other.

II.11   In the preceding paragraphs (II.2f.) we have noted the beginning of the erosion of traditional natural theology in the second half of the eighteenth century. The substance of Hume's views is that all metaphysical speculations about God and the soul ought, in the interests of genuine knowledge and its further accumulation, to be abandoned, on the grounds that such enquiries lie outside the scope of empirical testing, outside the scope of those veridical procedures which we ordinarily use in checking up within the area of 'fact and existence'. Hume's critique of metaphysics and natural theology is not only intrinsically important; it has been widely and powerfully influential in the area of twentieth-century positivism and empiricism. Indeed, no detraction from the achievements of twentieth-century empiricists is intended when the comment is made that much of their work has consisted of the re-interpretation of Hume's fundamental insights and the translation of these from the language of eighteenth-century psychology and epistemology into that of modern logic. To the views of several of these twentieth-century thinkers we now turn.

II.12 Classical Western empiricism received its greatest modern thrust in the second and third decades of the present century, with the foundation of the so-called Vienna Circle (which propagated its views in the international journal *Erkenntnis*), the publication of Ludwig Wittgenstein's *Tractatus Logico-Philosophicus*, and (in British circles) the publication of A. J. Ayer's *Language, Truth and Logic*. Members of the Vienna Circle openly admitted their indebtedness to their positivistic and empiricistic ancestors, notably Hume, Auguste Comte and Ernst Mach. The Humean influence is apparent in the Circle's attempt to limit meaningful discourse to the language of formal logic and mathematics (*a priori* analytic statements, necessarily and conventionally true), and of the natural sciences (*a posteriori* synthetic statements, verifiable or falsifiable by experience). Since the statements of metaphysics and natural theology did not fall into either class, they were frequently classified as *meaningless*. By this, members of the Circle meant that to mistake metaphysical issues for real factual issues worthy of human effort and enquiry was to commit oneself foolishly to a systematic waste of time and a dissipation of energy which were infinite, because *in principle* these issues were incapable of ever being settled.[13] To metaphysical statements there could not fruitfully be applied what later came to be known as the verification principle of logical positivism: 'the meaning of a (cognitive) statement is given by the method of its verification'.

II.13 Although not a formal member of the Circle, Wittgenstein corresponded with its members, was aware of its discussions, and came greatly to influence its views. The views of the 'early Wittgenstein' are to be found in his *Tractatus Logico-Philosophicus*.[14] The *Tractatus* distinguishes most sharply between the empirical sciences and philosophy: the difference is that whereas the sciences furnish us with propositions which can properly be regarded as either true or false, philosophy cannot. Hence Wittgenstein rejects the view of philosophy as a body of truths or doctrines which are unattainable by non-scientific methods; rather, philosophy is an activity, a way of life. It follows that the object of philosophy is *not the bringing to light of new facts*; its object is clarification, the clarification of the propositions, ideas and concepts brought to light by the methods of the natural sciences. Wittgenstein rejects as fallacious and pernicious the view that there are two competing or parallel theories or bodies of truth – science and philosophy. Rather, philosophy is a discipline which is parasitic upon the sciences: it is a higher-order activity, elucidating and clarifying the ideas arrived at by science; in doing so, it aims at being *therapeutic* by dissolving away our intellectual anxieties. It does so by demonstrating that certain problems (e.g. metaphysical ones) which vex us are but pseudo-problems. From this follows Wittgenstein's view of the history of philosophy: an examination of this brings to light the fundamental error of the classical philosophers, the failure to map the scope and limits of meaningful language. Having failed carefully to mark the boundary between meaningful and meaningless language, they frequently inadvertently crossed this frontier and *tried to say what cannot be said*. It is in this sense that we are to understand statements in *Tractatus* 4.003 such as, 'Most propositions and questions, that have been written about philosophical matters, are not false, but senseless (*unsinnig*).' Such questions and propositions 'result from the fact that we do not understand the logic of our language'. These views underlie Wittgenstein's rejection of metaphysics in the *Tractatus*.

II.14   One of Wittgenstein's aims in the *Tractatus* was to find a perfect language which accurately mirrors what is the case in the world. The key-concept here is that of a *proposition* (*Satz*), which in Wittgenstein's view *pictures* reality, or functions as a *model* of reality. Wittgenstein does not limit the term to written or spoken sentences, but includes within it gramophone records, musical scores and the like.[15] But if propositions are supposed to *picture* reality, how do we find out whether they are true or false?

> In order to discover whether the picture is true or false we must compare it with reality.
> It cannot be discovered from the picture alone whether it is true or false.
> There is no picture which is *a priori* true.[16]

But all such propositions are scientific and in no sense metaphysical ones. As Wittgenstein put it in the *Tractatus*:

> The totality of true propositions is the total natural science (or the totality of the natural sciences).
> Philosophy is not one of the natural sciences.[17]

Philosophical analysis (logic) demonstrates what *can* be said and what *cannot*. It thus *limits* language, which in turn sets a *limit* to thought; and this in turn sets a *limit* to the world.

> The limits of my language mean the limits of my world. Logic fills the world: the limits of the world are also its limits.[18]

The attempt of non-scientific metaphysics to describe the world is to be rejected in so far as metaphysical exploration claims to penetrate 'beyond' or 'behind' the world of everyday experience. Wittgenstein's views led to the expulsion of metaphysicians from areas in which they had, in his view, no right to dabble. The Darwinian theory of evolution, for example, is a completely scientific issue upon which the views of philosophers, *quâ* philosophers, are irrelevant.[19] And what of the *self*, discussed and theorized about by metaphysicians from Plato to recent times (II.10 above)? This is another matter for the scientist, namely, for the psychologist; and 'Psychology is no nearer related to philosophy, than is any other natural science.'[20]

II.15 In the *Tractatus*, Wittgenstein tackles the objection that to limit viable cognitive enquiries to scientific ones is completely to ignore the *great existential questions*, the 'riddle of life', the question of the meaning of human existence, and so on. He concedes the feeling of dissatisfaction we experience when questions of truth are restricted to science:

> We feel that if *all possible* scientific questions be answered, the problems of life have still not been touched at all. Of course there is then no question left, and just this is the answer.[21]

To see that this is so delivers us from needless anxiety; philosophy is a *therapeutic* activity:

> For an answer which cannot be expressed the question too cannot be expressed.
> *The riddle* does not exist.
> If a question can be put at all, then it can also be answered.[22]

Does this mean that there is in the *Tractatus* no place at all for *the religious*? In Wittgenstein's view, not quite. For he has much to say of the *mystical*, a conception despised by many of Wittgenstein's positivistic admirers, who took exception to passages in the *Tractatus* expounding its significance. What Wittgenstein actually has to say of it is rather obscure:

> There is indeed the inexpressible. This *shows* itself; it is the mystical.[23]
> Not *how* the world is, is the mystical, but *that* it is.[24]
> The solution of the riddle of life in space and time lies *outside* space and time.[25]
> God does not reveal himself *in* the world.[26]

If these words mean anything at all, prolonged contemplation of them leads us, in fear and trembling, to interpret them in this way. Something (apparently) *exists* apart from what is talked about in science, namely, the inexpressible, the mystical, *that* the world is, the solution of the riddle of life, 'God'; it appears to exist 'outside' the spatio-temporal world ('*outside* space and time', 'not . . . *in* the world'); this *shows* or reveals itself, we 'see' that it is so. From the analytic point of view of the *Tractatus* the only *linguistic* response to the mystical is silence, in the presence of the ineffable. In other words, the description and communication of the mystical are jobs which transcend the power of ordinary cognitive language. But this does not mean that in the *Tractatus* there is no room whatever for the *religious*. Indeed, it is not impossible to list those types of religion which are compatible with the teaching of the *Tractatus*. We might think, for example, of some extreme form of mysticism which holds that in some form of experience religious subjects are made immediately aware of something totally other-worldly and transcendent, an *ineffable* which totally transcends the limits of worldly language, and which therefore is quite incommunicable. Or again, we may think of some form of religion which completely rejects the notion of *transcendence* – a religious form which insists that religion has exclusively to do with man's spatio-temporal life, and which makes no reference to transcendent beings, states of affairs, or essences. And lastly, we may think of certain forms of extreme Barthian transcendentalism. Clearly, some Barthians would share the teaching of the *Tractatus*, welcoming it as a warranted attack on metaphysical theology. In doing so, they could fall back upon the typically Barthian teaching that in disclosing himself to man God miraculously creates within man the capacity to receive him, simultaneously imparting to man *a new language* which alone enables man to discourse intelligibly about God, a language which differs qualitatively from that used to describe the factual world of space and time which is analysed admirably in the *Tractatus*. Indeed, it appears to be no more historical accident that the heyday of Barthian fideism coincided with the heyday of European positivism (the nineteen-twenties and -thirties). Here is one point at any rate where Continental anti-metaphysical tendencies coincided with Anglo-Saxon ones.[27]

II.16   When we turn from Wittgenstein's *Tractatus* to the classical British exposition of logical positivism, A. J. Ayer's *Language, Truth and Logic*,[28] we find certain significant differences. For example, there is the close dependence of Ayer upon classical British empiricism, upon that of Hume especially. The most significant difference from our point of view is the complete absence in Ayer's book of anything like Wittgenstein's conception of the 'mystical': to the contrary, Ayer spelled out in grim and ruthless detail what he considered to be the extremely negative implications of logical positivism for religion. Before going on to glance at the anti-theological section of *Language, Truth and Logic*, we must note that to be found there is much that we have already considered: there is the attempt to confine significant propositions (to be found in different ways in Hume and Wittgenstein) to the two classes of logico-mathematical analytic ones and of the empirically verifiable ones of the natural sciences. Having ruled out metaphysical knowledge by doing so, Ayer considers that the rejection of religious knowledge is necessarily entailed by the dismissal of metaphysical truth-claims.[29]

II.17 The main anti-theological points of Ayer's book are fairly well known. The existence of a transcendent God cannot be 'proved', on the grounds that the certainty of any empirical demonstration depends upon the certainty of its premises. But empirical premises can always be doubted and can never be more than probable. Hence we can never 'prove' the existence of anything empirical.[30] Ayer makes a point of some importance in discussing the 'probability' which is sometimes alleged to adhere to theistic statements. Ayer insists that 'probable' existential propositions are empirical hypotheses in the sense that from them (and from other empirical hypotheses) may be deduced certain experiential propositions.[31] That is, a 'probable empirical hypothesis' must be able to contribute something (when taken with other empirical hypotheses) to the construction of experientially-testable *predictions*. If a, b and c, *then* d, e and f. But it is very difficult to see how theistic propositions can supply us with predictions about what will or will or not be the case if the propositions are true or false. Elsewhere, R. B. Braithwaite has made a similar point: 'It is,' writes Braithwaite, 'no valid criticism of the view that would treat God as an empirical concept entering into an explanatory hypothesis to say that God is not directly observable. No more is an electric field of force or a Schrödinger wave-function. There is no prima facie objection to regarding such a proposition as that there is a God who created and sustains the world as an explanatory scientific hypothesis.'[32] In this case, a symbol such as 'God' might appear as rather similar to highly abstract scientific concepts; the very significant difference is that these latter concepts, says Braithwaite, 'are given a meaning by the place they occupy in a deductive system consisting of hypotheses of different degrees of generality in which the least general hypotheses, deducible from the more general ones, are generalizations of observable facts.'[33] And he has little difficulty in showing that theistic propositions of a sophisticated type are not able to be tested by their ability to furnish their defenders with empirically-testable predictions.[34] In yet another way, empiricists have underscored the difference between metaphysical and scientific propositions.

II.18 Ayer sharply distinguishes his position from both atheism and agnosticism, on the grounds that both of these regard theistic propositions as significant, although they differ about the degree of probability or improbability which attaches to them.[35] Ayer's contention that all theistic propositions (without exception) are nonsensical implies that not only theism but negations of theism are nonsensical. Ayer has no quarrel with any religion (e.g. animism) in which the word 'God' is used to denote a spatio-temporal object. But he rightly points out that in the sophisticated theistic religions the word is used to refer to a non-spatio-temporal 'personal' being with super-empirical attributes, a notion which he rejects on the grounds of its empirical unintelligibility.[36] In the next paragraph we shall see how Ayer's rejection ties up with his rejection of the notion of a super-empirical personal *self*.

II.19 Ayer takes up the question of belief in immortality, and isolates for attention one theory upon which this belief is sometimes based.[37] This is the notion that within human personality there is an essential imperceptible something which is distinct from the body and which is capable of surviving death. Ayer rejects this notion as impossibly metaphysical, and to grasp his rejection we have to know something of his views of the self.[38] Ayer distinguishes his position from that of earlier empiricists (e.g. Hume, Mach) in that whereas they defended psychological and metaphysical views (e.g. Hume's 'bundle' theory), his own view tries to be exclusively *logical*. As a consistent positivist, Ayer was obliged to rule *all* metaphysical views (such as that the self is essentially an unobservable substantive ego) out of court as meaningless. Hence he adheres to the view that the self is a 'logical construction' out of actual and possible sense-experiences, and defines the link between sense experiences (which accounts for the continuity of experiences within the same person) as the material body. Hence he writes:

> ... just as I must define material things and my own self in terms of their empirical manifestations, so I must define other people in terms of their empirical manifestations – that is, in terms of the behaviour of their bodies, and ultimately in terms of sense-contents. The assumption that 'behind' these sense-contents there are entities which are not even in principle accessible to my observation can have no more significance for me than the admittedly metaphysical assumption that such entities 'underlie' the sense-contents which constitute material things for me, or my own self. And thus I find that I have as good a reason to believe in the existence of other people as I have to believe in the existence of material things. For in each case my hypothesis is verified by the occurrence in my sense-history of the appropriate series of sense-contents.[39]

Although this subject was introduced originally in connection with a certain kind of belief in immortality, it has intrinsic importance for contemporary epistemology of religion, and we shall have to give it a much fuller treatment at a later point (VI).

II.20 Ayer concludes his attack on religion, on empiricistic grounds, by making some further points. He insists, for example, that his view rules out of court any meaningful clash between science and religion, on the grounds that whereas the propositions of the former, being empirically verifiable, are perfectly meaningful, the propositions of the latter, being empirically unverifiable, are simply not genuine propositions at all.[40] And he follows the example of Ernst Mach in arguing that science, in rationally exploring the world, makes it a much less mysterious and much more predictable and hence more manipulable place; scientific exploration is therefore the enemy of that religious awe which springs, in Ayer's view, from man's existence in an alien, because unknown, world.[41] When Ayer comes to discuss *mysticism* his account differs sharply from the Wittgensteinian account of the 'mystical'.[42] While protesting that he does not wish to deny *a priori* the mystic's claim to discover truth in his own way, he quarrels with him at that point where the mystic insists that what he apprehends in his experience is *absolutely* incapable of being mediated in propositions. Ayer insists that the mystic's refusal at this point reveals that what he claims to 'know' or 'apprehend' is unsubstantiated on the grounds that the utter lack of objective reference reveals that this 'knowledge' has nothing whatever to say about the external spatio-temporal world. He concludes therefore that the claims of the mystic are revelatory only of the interior state of his own mind. Ayer's discussion of religious experience is pertinent to much that we had to say in the first chapter of post-Schleiermacher trends in modern German theology. The kernel of Ayer's contribution is that there is vast difference between, on the one hand, a claim to experience 'a peculiar kind of sense-content' (we might think, perhaps, of a feeling of religious awe, or of Schleiermacher's feeling of absolute dependence) and, on the other, a claim to experience God. He has no quarrel with the first sort of claim; his objection to the second sort is rooted in the fact that the word 'God' carries connotations of *transcendence* with it, a conception which immediately carries us beyond the area of possible or actual worldly experience. For an empiricist like Ayer this means, of course, that we have entered the area of unverifiable and unfalsifiable nonsense, the area of metaphysics. What is illuminating here is that whereas post-Schleiermacher anti-metaphysical theologians have loudly insisted that that dimension of God's being which lies beyond religious experience (however defined) can be of no interest or concern to genuine theology, Ayer would sharply disagree. He would insist that to talk intelligibly about 'God' necessarily involves one in talking about God's *otherness*; and he would interpret their refusal to discuss this theologically as an intolerable equation of 'experiencing God' with 'experiencing peculiar kinds of sense-contents'. In other words, anti-metaphysical theologies based entirely and exclusively upon religious *experience* (however defined) provide us, at the end of the day, with a wealth of interesting knowledge about the experiences of religious subjects. And an empiricist like Ayer, while freely conceding that such experiences may be interesting, is forced to the conclusion that such knowledge in the last analysis merely augments our information about *human beings*. As we said above, the price which *exclusively* experiential theologians have to pay for their complete exclusion of metaphysics from theology is a high one (I.20).

II.21 The second edition of Ayer's *Language, Truth and Logic* was published in 1946. It was as true then of England as it was of Continental Europe that, in Ninian Smart's words, 'Natural theology is the Sick Man of Europe'. The view taken then of the viability of natural theology in the second half of the twentieth century was pretty much the same in Basel or Bonn as in Oxford or Cambridge, and for not dissimilar reasons. On both sides of the English Channel, the discussions of metaphysical theology which had been going for a couple of centuries had seriously undermined the confidence of Europeans in any resuscitation of the discipline. Metaphysical theology, it was felt, took us beyond experience into some unfathomable and unchartable area of 'things-in-themselves'; with metaphysics we had apparently left verifiability and falsifiability far behind, and had apparently committed ourselves to some time-consuming programme the satisfactory conclusion of which literally no one could foresee. The detailed and tough-minded comparison of science and metaphysics had clearly shown that whereas issues and problems in the former were closely tied up with viable experimental procedures and programmes, those in the latter could never be solved in any such way. In the meantime the process of secularization (culminating in the discovery and exploitation of nuclear energy) had been operating for three or four centuries; more and more confidence had been generated in man's ability to interpret and explain the world in this-worldly terms. Throughout these processes, as we have seen, modern philosophy and theology had heavily underscored at point after point the centrality and cruciality of one theological issue above all others – the issue of the *transcendence* of God, of

God understood as a being who exists somehow 'beyond' the spatio-temporal world. This can be seen by examining the writings of such a mixed Anglo-Continental group as Hume, Kant, Schleiermacher, Ritschl, Barth, Bultmann, Russell, Wittgenstein and Ayer. In the post-war world, while Continental theologians were on the whole content to continue dealing with this by confining theological data within the boundaries of *experience* (e.g. Bultmann, etc.), or by relying exclusively on some other-worldly revelation (e.g. Barth, etc.), many Anglo-Saxons have continued to take the problem of natural theology (or of the decline of natural theology) with much greater seriousness. This kind of position can be examined in some detail in a paper such as Ninian Smart's 'Revelation, Reasons and Religions',[43] where it is persuasively argued that the alternative to the breakdown of classical metaphysical theology is not theological irrationalism. Rather, Smart wishes 'to consider whether there is a middle way between traditional natural theology and some simple appeal to revelation (or to any other authority)'.[44] The fact that English thinkers could still speak as optimistically as this about natural theology in 1961, in a volume entitled *Prospect for Metaphysics*, was due partly at least to a revolution which had been going on for some little time in post-war English philosophy. This was closely tied up with the later work of Ludwig Wittgenstein, to which we now briefly turn.

II.22   The later work of Wittgenstein is to be found largely in the posthumously published *Philosophical Investigations*.[45] The *Investigations* reveals Wittgenstein's feelings of dissatisfaction with many of the key-doctrines of the *Tractatus*. Particularly, Wittgenstein rejects its 'picture-theory' of language, its fundamental conviction that the job of language is to picture or reflect factual states of affairs in the world, and that the analyst's aim is to uncover that linguistic *essence* which underlies the actual uses of language, in the process distinguishing between meaningful and meaningless statements and propositions. In this view, language is divided into two basic significant types – the logico-mathematical analytic and the empirically verifiable synthetic type whose clearest expression is to be found in the natural sciences. The Wittgenstein of the *Investigations* abandons this view, and expounds the novel doctrine that language is very much more complex than this; he speaks of it as a group of varied 'language-games' (*Sprachspiele*) which share family resemblances. In order to find our way around these language-games, we must think of words, not as the names of empirically identifiable objects, but as *tools*.[46] And the only way of understanding and distinguishing between tools is to enquire for their *use*. Wittgenstein's conception of the 'multiplicity of language-games' is to be found in *Investigations* 23: 'It is interesting to compare the multiplicity of tools in language and of the ways they are used, the multiplicity of kinds of word and sentence, with what logicians have said about the structure of language. (Including the author of the *Tractatus Logico-Philosophicus*.)' Each *use* of language can only be explored in its context, which includes acting as well as speaking: 'I shall . . . call the whole, consisting of language and the actions into which it is woven, the "language-game".'[47] In this later view of Wittgenstein, the *meaning* of a word is not something that can be appreciated independently of its *use*; rather, its meaning *is* its use. He illustrates his point from chess: the *meanings* of words like 'pawn' and 'king' can only be learned by seeing how they are *used* in a specific game, and this is true of the words of language-games other than chess.

II.23   The later Wittgenstein holds that philosophy is a *descriptive* discipline:

> Philosophy may in no way interfere with the actual use of language; it can in the end only describe it.
> For it cannot give it any foundation either.
> It leaves everything as it is.
> It also leaves mathematics where it is, and no mathematical discovery can advance it.[48]

This point should make over-confident theologians beware. For it is clear that the Wittgenstein of the *Investigations* did *not* reject the logic of logico-mathematical analytic and empirically verifiable synthetic propositions as this is set forth in the *Tractatus*. The *Investigations* merely rejected the view of the *Tractatus* that these two types are the *only* types of significant language, teaching rather that there was an immense multiplicity of language-games, *including* those of mathematics and the physical sciences. The later Wittgenstein disapproved of the *Tractatus*'s programme of *reductive* analysis (the reduction of significant types to those of mathematics and physics). But nowhere did Wittgenstein soften the demand for veridical procedures with regard to factual assertions. It would be fatal for theologians to imagine that in post-Wittgensteinian analytic philosophy this demand had been quietly dropped! If theologians believe that their propositions are statements about reality (what is the case), that they are in some sense or another *factual*, they cannot ignore the question of the precise logic of these propositions. If this logic is not that of analytic statements nor that of empirically verifiable ones, then *what precisely is the logic that underlies them* (II.27)?

II.24 Another similarity between the two main works of Wittgenstein is that both in their own way adhere to the view of philosophy as a therapeutic and anxiety-alleviating discipline (cf. II.13 above). 'Philosophy,' as defined in the *Investigations*, 'is a battle against the bewitchment of our intelligence by means of language.'[49] 'The results of philosophy are the uncovering of one or another piece of plain nonsense and of bumps that the understanding has got by running its head against the limits of language.'[50] Philosophy thus alleviates our anxiety: 'What is your aim in philosophy? – To show the fly the way out of the fly-bottle.'[51] Wittgenstein describes how this may be done as bringing 'words back from their metaphysical to their everyday use'.[52] Thus when philosophers perplex us by discussing words like 'being' or 'object', when they try to find what their *essential* meaning is, Wittgenstein's therapeutic advice is to bring such words back from their metaphysical to their everyday use, and ask: 'Is the word ever actually used in this way in the language-game which is its original home?'[53] Donald Hudson gives an interesting application of this point to theological propositions.[54] He suggests that the demand that theological propositions be straightforwardly empirically verifiable (or be rejected as meaningless) is to treat them as straightforward scientific hypotheses, a perplexing confusion which can only be dissolved away by enquiring about the way such propositions are originally used in the language-game or form of life in which they had their origin – we might think here, for example, of the language-game of religion.[55]

II.25 Another point made by Wittgenstein is of importance for understanding post-analytic philosophical theology. 'Thinking is not an incorporeal process which lends life and sense to speaking, and which it would be possible to detach from speaking. . . .'[56] That is, thinking is not some ghostly, hidden process that *underlies* language, which lies concealed 'behind' or 'beyond' speech, which gives rise to speech. Rather, speech 'is' thinking; thinking must necessarily issue in language; thinking involves speech, so that the former is inconceivable without the latter. It is true that this is suggestive of behaviourism, yet what Wittgenstein is really trying to stress is the indissolubly close connection between thinking and language, between thought and words, between concepts and concrete symbols. This is worth noting, if only in view of the exasperation shown by some towards analytic philosophers on the grounds of the latter's 'obsession with language' or 'linguistic madness', an exasperation not uncommon in certain theological circles in the United States. For when the analyst (and the post-analytic philosopher of religion) directs his attention closely to, for instance, theological words, sentences and propositions, he is simultaneously, *pari passu*, dealing with theological thought, conceptualization and persuasion, since the latter are not, according to the Wittgensteinian viewpoint, some ghostly, hidden processes which eventually 'produce' the former. Rather, the former in some sense 'are' the latter. It is well to grasp this point before dealing with the works of strictly linguistic philosophers of religion, such as Ian T. Ramsey.

II.26 Wittgenstein's influence on modern philosophy has been both broad and deep. Probably his most significant legacy to pure philosophy has been the analysis of ordinary language. His influence on philosophy of religion has also been of some significance. The views expressed in the *Philosophical Investigations* have been instrumental in the lifting of what H. J. Paton has called the *linguistic veto* imposed upon theology by logical positivism.[57] It is not difficult to enumerate those elements in the later Wittgenstein's thought which have played a significant part in the lifting of the ban, and in opening the door, however cautiously, to admit some new possibility of metaphysical theology. We may perhaps list some questions which were opened up by these post-war advances in philosophy. If there was a multiplicity of language-games (each with it own 'form of life'), then ought not critical attention be paid to the language-game of theology and to the form of life in which it originates? If words are to be understood as tools which we use rather than as names which we apply, ought not theologians now to devote themselves to an examination of those ways in which their key words are *used* in the form of life and language-game of religion? Theological self-confidence was re-kindled by Wittgenstein's teaching that philosophy was essentially a descriptive discipline and that it 'it may in no way interfere with the actual use of language' and that 'it leaves everything as it is' (II.23). This, it was felt, generated an entirely different kind of philosophical atmosphere from that in which theologians worked in the heyday of the older positivism. The Wittgensteinian notion that philosophy understood as analysis is a therapeutic activity in which muddles and confusions are cleared up led some theologians (the classic example of whom is Ian T. Ramsey) to hold that the new analytic techniques supplied theologians with indispensable and long overdue means whereby the jungle of theological verbiage might be tackled, with a view to bringing some order into a rather undisciplined and untidy theological garden.

II.27 The ban had been lifted and the door opened, however cautiously. In a rather aphoristic remark, Wittgenstein had defined theology as 'grammar' (*Investigations*, 373). This meant that theologians had been given the opportunity of elucidating the logic and rules underlying their particular language-game, an opportunity given equally, of course, to moralists, metaphysicians and aestheticians. No longer was metaphysical theology ruled out of court *a priori* as meaningless, simply because its propositions were not of the same logical type as those of mathematics or physics. It is understandable, therefore, that there should appear a considerable volume of theological writings devoted to the question of the logic underlying religious beliefs, ways of life, activities and discourse. Hence we had explorations and elucidations of the logic of prayer, of worship, of decision, and of self-involvement. In a critical survey by Frederick Ferré of possible theological responses to the new philosophical trends were the logics of analogy, of obedience and of encounter. [58] But, as we noted above, the door had been opened *cautiously*. The reason for this caution has already been hinted at in II.23. The new functional analysis did not at all reject the hard-won lessons gained during the positivistic era with regard to statements claiming to be informative about states of affairs, about 'how things are', for which certain veridical procedures had been demanded. In other words, in the case of truth-claims the 'logic of verification' was not abandoned by functional analysts. It followed therefore that theologians who still wished to maintain that theology made truth-claims were required to tread cautiously, in the sense that they were required to take cognizance of the analysis of cognitive propositions elucidated by the older-style positivism. Theologians claiming that theological propositions were cognitive would henceforth be required to demonstrate most carefully *in what sense* they were cognitive, and to relate their fundamental logic to the logic of other (non-theological) propositions making truth-claims. James Alfred Martin Jr has made this point neatly:

> ... the strong counterstatements of the *Investigations* should not lead to the conclusion that the *Tractatus* is not an important work about an important 'game', or that it is not important to be as clear as possible about how a language employing its rules is like or differs from other languages. Sentences *are* used for more purposes than stating facts; but that fact alone does not explain or justify the appearance of, or implicit claim to, fact-stating in other uses. If theologians, in particular, go on to justify theo-

logical language on the grounds that it is all part of a 'theological language game', and therefore can be judged only in terms of internal consistency or obedience to self-generated rules, they must be reminded that there is a continuing obligation to say where there is congruence with other games, and on what grounds and at what points they would claim autonomy.[59]

II.28 It is therefore not altogether surprising that certain scholars, exploring the logic of religion in the years following the publication of the *Investigations*,[60] utterly abandoned the claim that the purpose of religious language and symbolism is to make factual truth-claims. For example, Wittgenstein's Cambridge colleague R. B. Braithwaite, writing in 1955, rejected the truth-claims of religious language on grounds strongly reminiscent of those advanced by logical positivists.[61] Braithwaite went on to explore the logic of religious belief and utterance in terms of the 'use principle' to be found in the *Philosophical Investigations*: 'the meaning of any statement is given by the way in which it is used'.[62] His explanation of the logical status of this principle is illuminating and ought to be well pondered by theologians. In adopting the use principle, says Braithwaite, 'there is no desertion from the spirit of empiricism'. This is because 'the older verificational principle is subsumed under the new principle: the use of an empirical statement derives from the fact that the statement is empirically verifiable, and the logical-positivist thesis of the "linguistic" character of logical and mathematical statement can be equally well, if not better, expressed in terms of their uses than of their method of verification.'[63]

II.29 Nevertheless, certain scholars in the Anglo-Saxon tradition believed that religious truth-claims could not be so summarily abandoned, and that some attempt to substantiate these might be made while taking full cognizance of the developments which had occurred in British philosophy in recent decades. We turn in the next chapter to one such attempt in Anglo-Saxon theological circles. But before we can understand the issues involved in this we must examine several philosophical developments which were eventually seen to be relevant by theologians. One of these is to be found in Wittgenstein's *Philosophical Investigations* itself.

NOTES

1. For this subject, consult C. F. von Weizsäcker, *The Relevance of Science: Creation and Cosmogony*, London, 1964, especially chapter 10, 'What is Secularization?'.

2. *Dialogues Concerning Natural Religion*, ed. Norman Kemp Smith, Oxford, 1935, p. 224.

3. *Dialogues*, VI.

4. *Dialogues*, X and XI.

5. *Enquiries*, ed. L. A. Selby-Bigge, Oxford, 1966, p. 165.

6. ' "Universes," as C. S. Peirce remarked, "are not so plentiful as blackberries",' quoted by Antony Flew, *God and Philosophy*, London, 1966, p. 74.

7. The relevant sections of Hume's writing are 'Of the Immortality of the Soul', and 'Of Personal Identity', in *A Treatise of Human Nature*, Pt. IV.

8. *Treatise*, Dolphin Books Edition, New York, 1961, p. 213; Hume here comes close to using the terminology of later logical positivism, which asserted that metaphysical enquiries and propositions are *meaningless*. Cf. below, II.12.

9. *Op. cit.*, p. 217.

10. *Op. cit.*, p. 229, italics mine.

11. In the 'Appendix' of the *Treatise*, Hume writes of the problem: 'For my part, I must plead the privilege of the sceptic, and confess that this difficulty is too hard for my understanding', *op. cit.*, p. 560.

12. *Op. cit.*, p. 228.

13. It is interesting to note though that one of the original members of the Circle, Rudolf Carnap, suggested that metaphysics originally served as the 'expression of the general attitude of a person towards life (*Lebenseinstellung, Lebensgefühl*)'. He further suggested that metaphysics originated in mythology, and that metaphysics is an inadequate substitute for art; 'metaphysicians are musicians without musical ability'. The wickedness of metaphysics is that its immaculate grammatical form deludes its adherents into believing that it really is about states of affairs, that it really is saying something; see Carnap's 'The Elimination of Metaphysics Through the Logical Analysis of Language' in *Logical Positivism*, ed. A. J. Ayer, Glencoe, Illinois, 1959, pp. 60–81. And Carl Hempel remarks that many of the formulations of traditional metaphysics are rich 'in non-cognitive import by virtue of their emotive appeal or the moral inspiration they offer', *op. cit.*, p. 108.

14. German/English text, London, 1922.

15. *Tractatus*, 4.014.

16. *Op. cit.*, 2.223–2.225.

17. *Ibid.*, 4.11 and 4.111.

18. 5.6–5.61(I).

19. 4.1122.

20. 4.1121(I).

21. 6.52–6.521(I).

22. 6.5.

23. 6.522.

24. 6.44.
25. 6.4312.
26. 6.432.
27. See my paper 'The Contemporary Crisis in English Academic Theology', *Canadian Journal of Theology*, vol. XIV (1968), No. 2: 'Science was in, religion and metaphysics were out. It has been observed that, so far as the impossibility of rational theology was concerned, there was a large measure of agreement between Ayer and Wittgenstein on the one hand, and Karl Barth and his disciples on the other. . . . If not speculative reason, then biblical revelation!'
28. First published 1936; second revised edition 1946. References in what follows are to the 1946 editions.
29. *Language, Truth and Logic*, p. 114.
30. *Ibid.*, pp. 114–15.
31. *Ibid.*, p. 115.
32. *An Empiricist's View of the Nature of Religious Belief*, Cambridge, 1955, pp. 5–6.
33. *Ibid.*, p. 5.
34. *Ibid.*, pp. 6–8.
35. *Language, Truth and Logic*, pp. 115–16; in terms which we used to describe Hume's position, to enter into a discussion of the strengths and weaknesses of atheism and agnosticism would be to commit oneself to an infinitely time-consuming and energy-dissipating programme, all to no avail.
36. *Ibid.*, p. 116.
37. *Ibid.*, p. 117.
38. *Ibid.*, chapter VII, 'The Self and the Common World': with what follows compare what was said of Hume in II.10 and also of Wittgenstein in II.14. It is only fair to state that Ayer has changed his mind about much of the content of chapter VII since it was published in 1946.
39. *Ibid.*, p. 130.
40. *Ibid.*, p. 117.
41. *Ibid.*
42. *Ibid.*, pp. 118–19; cf. II.15 above.
43. In *Prospect for Metaphysics*, pp. 80–92.
44. *Op. cit.*, p. 80; from the same point of view, Howard Root's 'Metaphysics and Religious Belief' in the same volume (pp. 64–79) is also illuminating.
45. Oxford, 1953; cf. the 'preliminary studies' for the *Investigations*, *The Blue and Brown Books*, Oxford, 1958.
46. *Investigations*, 11f.
47. *Ibid.*, 7; cf. 23: 'the *speaking* of language is part of an activity, or of a form of life'.
48. *Ibid.*, 124.
49. *Ibid.*, 109.
50. 119.
51. 309.
52. 116.
53. *Ibid.*

54. In *Ludwig Wittgenstein*, Makers of Contemporary Theology Series, London, 1968, pp. 55–56.

55. See V. 3f. below, where we shall attempt to describe other language-games which give rise to theistic propositions.

56. *Investigations*, 339; see 341f.

57. *The Modern Predicament*, London, 1955, chapter II.

58. *Language, Logic and God*, chapters 6–8.

59. *The New Dialogue Between Philosophy and Theology*, London, 1966, p. 110.

60. Part I of the volume was completed by 1945, and Part II was composed between 1947 and 1949 (Editors' note in the *Investigations*). But Wittgenstein's views were well known before this through his University teaching and through the materials circulated in the Blue and Brown Books in the nineteen-thirties.

61. *An Empiricist's View of the Nature of Religious Belief*, pp. 4–10.

62. *Ibid.*, p. 10.

63. *Ibid.*

III

'SEEING AS' IN THEORY AND PRACTICE

III.1 Towards the end of Wittgenstein's *Investigations* there is to be found an analysis of the verb 'to see'.[1] Here Wittgenstein develops the concept of 'seeing as'. If we contemplate a certain picture, for example, we can see it *as* one thing or *as* another.

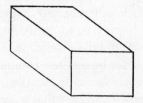

This picture, says Wittgenstein, can be seen *as* a glass cube, or *as* an inverted open box, or *as* a wire frame of that shape, or *as* three boards forming a solid angle. Wittgenstein insists that we do not merely *see*, we *see as*, and what we *see* something *as* depends upon how we *interpret* it. Hence *seeing* necessarily involves *interpretation*. Wittgenstein gives the example of the 'duck-rabbit', the image which can be seen *as* a rabbit or *as* a duck.[2] He introduces the conception of *aspect*: we might see a thing for some time under a certain *aspect*; then another *aspect* 'dawns' upon us, and we see something quite different. It is possible for me to see an object or picture for a considerable length of time under one *aspect*; then, coming to see it quite differently, I might exclaim, 'I saw it quite differently, I should never have recognized it!'[3] A *change* has taken place, but it is difficult to say in what the change consists.

III.2 Wittgenstein makes a point whose significance for the epistemology of religion we shall develop at a later point when he writes of the picture of the duck-rabbit's head: 'Nor has the head seen like *this* the slightest similarity to the head seen like *this* – although they are congruent.'[4] The point here is that when two observers differ as to what it is they are seeing (one a rabbit, the other a duck; one a glass cube, the other an inverted box), it is nevertheless true that they are seeing the *same facts*, the same paper, the identical arrangement of lines and dots inscribed upon it. In this sense, there is no *factual* difference between them; one does not see a fact (or facts) which are concealed from the other. And yet, both see the totality *as* quite different things; *aspectually*, their two visions are quite different. Paradoxically, there is *one* set of facts, open to all, yet *two* different pictures. Wittgenstein raises the difficult question as to the nature of the difference: '. . . what is different: my impression? my point of view? – Can I say?'[5] If one tries to clarify the difference between the two observers contemplating the same picture by asking one to make a model of what he sees *now* compared to what he saw *before*, the two models are factually identical. 'If I represent it by means of an exact copy – and isn't that a good representation of it? – no change is shown.'[6] Hence Wittgenstein can say that ' "Seeing as . . ." is not part of perception. And for that reason it is like seeing and again not like.'[7] Wittgenstein admits that *thought* does enter into the difference: 'If you are looking at the object, you need not think of it; but if you are having the visual experience . . . you are also *thinking* of what you see.'[8] Wittgenstein's account of 'seeing as' in *Investigations* 197[e]f. brings home to us just how complex the process of *seeing* is. 'The concept of "seeing" makes a tangled impression': 'How completely ragged what we see can appear.'[9] 'The concept of a representation of what is seen, like that of a copy, is very *elastic* and so *together with it* is the concept of what is seen.'[10] Hopefully, enough has been said to enable us to proceed to the application of the concept of 'seeing as' to the problem of metaphysical theology.

III.3 The fruitfulness of Wittgenstein's analysis can perhaps be appreciated if we apply it to the situation where what is contemplated is not some single object or other, but *the world taken* *as a whole*, or, more satisfactorily, *one's entire experience of the world taken as a whole*. The proposal is that the world, too, which we contemplate can be seen *as* one thing or *as* some altogether different thing. This insight has led some Wittgensteinians to the view that this is the process which is essentially involved in the construction of metaphysical schemes. The metaphysician, it has been suggested, is at pains to elucidate a helpful, illuminating, clarifying, over-all view of the world, as he sees it.[11] Here we have the definition of metaphysics as a conspectus, map, grid, slant, or model;[12] as a model, pattern, grid or framework upon which we rationally arrange and structure our worldly experience *taken as a whole*, into some meaningful, organic unity; as a rational *synopsis* of all our experience. Or we may consider the notion as that of metaphysics as essentially the linguistic formulation or representation of a conspectus of or slant on the world which appears to the viewer to possess explanatory value, and, it may be, heuristic significance. Alternatively, the notion can usefully be described as that of metaphysics as an overall, meaningful *projection* of the world, a cartographical term which links up with what we have to say below of metaphysics as a form of cosmic *map-making*. We cannot here tackle the large and difficult question of whether or not metaphysicians of the past were doing this sort of thing, independently of whether or not they were aware of it. It is enough for our purposes if we recognize that if this method of doing metaphysics could be shown to be viable, it would be relevant to how we have already defined natural theology, as 'the rational construction of *a vision of the world as a whole* . . . which is the sole explanation of a universe of experience which would otherwise be left extremely obscure, problematic and unclear' (I.2). We have already learned from Wittgenstein something of the complexity of those differences which divide those who see things *as* one thing rather than *as* another; rather, therefore, than explore this complexity in the abstract, it might make for greater clarity if we explore it in the context of a definite, concrete attempt to demonstrate what is involved in seeing the entire world *as* one thing rather than *as* another. To this, a classic attempt, we now turn.

III.4 The attempt is to be found in the work of Wittgenstein's successor John Wisdom, in the form of a parable whose context is Wisdom's celebrated paper *Gods*.[13] The text of the parable is as follows:

> *How it is that an explanatory hypothesis, such as the existence of God, may start by being experimental and gradually become something quite different can be seen from the following story:*
>
> Two people return to their long-neglected garden and find among the weeds a few of the old plants surprisingly vigorous. One says to the other, 'It must be that a gardener has been coming and doing something about these plants.' Upon inquiry they find that no neighbour has ever seen anyone at work in their garden. The first man says to the other, 'He must have worked while people slept.' The other says 'No, someone would have heard him and besides, anybody who cared about the plants would have kept down these weeds.' The first man says 'Look at the way these are arranged. There is purpose and a feeling for beauty here. I believe that someone comes, someone invisible to mortal eyes. I believe that the more carefully we look the more we shall find confirmation of this.' They examine the garden ever so carefully and sometimes they come on new things suggesting that a gardener comes and sometimes they come on new things suggesting the contrary and even that a malicious person has been at work. Besides examining the garden carefully they also study what happens to gardens left without attention. Each learns all the other learns about this and about the garden. Consequently, when after all this, one says 'I still believe a gardener comes' while the other says 'I don't' their different words now reflect no difference as to what they have found in the garden, no difference as to what they would find in the garden if they looked further and no difference about how fast untended gardens fall into disorder. At this stage, in this context, the gardener hypothesis has ceased to be experimental, the difference between one who accepts and one who rejects it is now not a matter of the one expecting something the other does not expect. What is the difference between them? The one says 'A gardener comes unseen and unheard. He is manifested only in his works with which we are all familiar', the other says 'There is no gardener' and with this difference in what they say about the gardener goes a difference in how they feel towards the garden, in spite of the fact that neither expects anything of it which the other does not expect.
>
> But is this the whole difference between them – that the one calls the garden by one name and feels one way towards it, while the other calls it by another name and feels in another way towards it? And if this is what the difference has become then is it any longer appropriate to ask 'Which is right?' or 'Which is reasonable?'.[14]

III.5 The point reiterated by Wisdom in his writings on religion, that 'The existence of God is not an experimental issue in the way it was'.[15], is greatly significant. The conviction that theism is an issue which cannot conceivably be dealt with in terms of observations, tests, predictions and the like, is one of the main lessons taught by empiricists from Hume to Ayer. The conviction led most of them to say, as we noted, that therefore *the theistic issue is time-wasting nonsense.* But Wisdom does not think so; he is convinced that many significant issues (including the theistic one) not amenable to experimental reasoning and testing are nevertheless real, significant issues which can be discussed rationally, and about which people can quite reasonably make decisions leading to responsible action. Wisdom's parable shows that in his view the theistic issue is closely tied up with seeing the world *as* one thing rather than *as* another. In this issue 'all the facts are in'; there are no facts concealed from either of the observers; neither of them can have any hope that one day the difference between them may be finally resolved as outstanding disputes in chemistry or archaeology may one day be resolved, by the discovery of fresh facts. So (in the first instance at any rate), no factual difference divides believer from un-believer.[16] One selects and interprets one group of facts as evidence for theism, the other emphasizes a different constellation of facts as counter-evidence for theism. At this stage the theist may well react hostilely and complain that this way of approaching theism is thoroughly naturalistic – that theism and atheism in Wisdom's view appear to be merely a matter of subjective taste and feeling ('. . . with this difference in what they say about the garden goes a difference in how they *feel* towards the garden . . .'). But it is not so; there is, in Wisdom's view, a great deal more to the difference than that.

III.6   Wisdom formulates a formal principle for making decisions in such cases in the following terms: 'A question is a real, meaningful question if either it can be answered by observation or it can be answered by demonstration from premises which are either self-evident or obtained by describing what we have observed.'[17] By ascribing meaningfulness to questions to which . answers can be found by 'describing what we have observed', Wisdom hopes to show that theological questions are real and

significant questions rather than time-consuming blind alleys.
One point he makes is that sometimes scientists do something of
the kind in their theory-making: 'Newton with his doctrine of
gravitation gave us a so much greater apprehension of nature
not so much because he told us what we would or would not
see . . ., but because he enabled us to see anew a thousand
familiar incidents.'[18] Hence Wisdom rejects as altogether inadequate and unsatisfactory the empiricistic principle of which we
have heard so much above: 'A statement hasn't really a meaning unless it can be settled either by observation or by the sort of
definite procedure by which questions of mathematics or logic
can be settled, otherwise it isn't a real, meaningful question but
verbal, emotive, or nonsensical.'[19] The reasons for Wisdom's
rejection are twofold: first, the sheer quantity of *inescapable,
significant human situations* which cannot be handled in experimental and observational terms, and, second, the fact that there
are, in Wisdom's view, certain *epistemological techniques* which
can be elucidated in order to settle these non-experimental
truth-claiming issues. We must deal with each of these two in
turn.

III.7 One type of inescapably significant human situation
much discussed by Wisdom is that which takes place in the *law-
court*. For example, in *Gods* 6.5[20] Wisdom argues that in such
courts the fact that disagreeing counsel are agreed as to the facts
(which are open to all) does not at all mean that the issues to be
settled are not real ones which must be settled in the public
interest. No one in his senses would describe such a non-experimental disagreement as metaphysical and therefore nonsensical,
involving participants in endless time-wasting. An attempt must
be made to *interpret* the facts, to find a significant *pattern* in them.
The logic involved in resolving non-experimental differences is
reflected also in the ruling required of a judge in a law-court,[21] a
matter which no one but the most unworldly academic or
the irresponsible would describe as time-wasting or energy-
dissipating. Once again, the judge is required to *interpret*,
to find a significant *pattern* in, what has been disclosed to all.

Elsewhere, we find Wisdom returning for examples to the legal sphere:

> To hint that when we are concerned with questions which are still un-answered when we have left no stone unturned, no skid mark unmeasured, then thinking is no use, is to forget that when the facts are agreed upon we must still hear argument before we give judgment. To hint that, when argument cannot show that in the usual usage of language the correct answer is Yes or No it shows us nothing, is to forget that such argument is in such a case just as necessary and just as valuable for an apprehension of the case before us as it is in those cases when it happens that we can express that greater apprehension in a word – Guilty, Not Guilty, Mad, Not Mad, Negligent, Not Negligent, Cruel, Not Cruel.[22]

To argue otherwise, and on traditionally empiricistic grounds to urge non-participation in such non-experimental matters, is 'to denigrate the very modes of thought that we need most when most we need to think.'[23] And elsewhere we find this:

> The facts agreed upon, still a question is before the bar of reason as when, the facts agreed upon, still a question comes before a court. 'Was there negligence or was there not?' To such a question the maybe answer is 'Yes', maybe the answer is 'No', maybe the answer is neither 'Yes' nor 'No'. But the question is not beyond the scope of reason.[24]

Elsewhere, there is a passage in which Wisdom returns to the same point in the form of a dialogue with an imaginary sceptical philosopher of law, who argues that legal questions are really decisions about wise, expedient action, rather than questions of truth. The gist of Wisdom's conclusion in the dialogue is contained in these words:

> 'Argument must be heard. Argument which is not merely any psychological procedure which obtains a certain result, but a procedure in which we set this by that, and that by this, so as to see more clearly than we did at first what it was that happened, and then and only then to act. To describe such a procedure as a process primarily of persuasion to a line of action, to say that a search for the truth is not of the essence of the procedure, is to say what is dangerous, defamatory and false.[25]

III.8 Other significant human situations are brought forward by Wisdom in support of his contention that basically non-experimental questions may nevertheless be real, meaningful ones. There is, for instance, the case of two people contemplating a picture or natural scene. 'One says "Excellent" or "Beautiful" or "Divine"; the other says "I don't see it".... And yet surely each sees what the other sees. It isn't that one can see part of the picture which the other can't. So the difference is not one as to the facts.' Yet, the disputants do not regard the difference between them as a matter of arbitrary or contrary taste. Rather is it that one regards the other as *blind*, while the latter regards the former as seeing what is not there. The same applies to similarly aesthetic situations, such as listening to a piece of music. 'The difference as to whether a God exists . . . is . . . like a difference as to whether there is beauty in a thing.'[26]

III.9 We enquire now about the *logic* involved in deciding about non-experimental truth-claims, an enquiry which leads to the question of the relation between this logic and factuality, an issue of crucial importance (cf. III.5 above). First, there is the enquiry about the logic involved. Negatively, Wisdom insists that it is 'not a *chain* of demonstrative reasoning', 'not that of a chain of deductive reasoning as in a mathematical calculation'.[27] Rather, the persuader goes over his case presenting and re-presenting features of it 'which *severally co-operate* in favour of the conclusion'. The reasons, says Wisdom, 'are like the legs of a chair, not the links of a chain'; the reasoning involved 'is not *vertically* extensive but *horizontally* extensive'. The logic, in his view, is 'a matter of the cumulative effect of several independent premises, not of the repeated transformation of one or two'. The premises are 'severally inconclusive'; hence the logic involves us in 'weighing the cumulative effect of one group of severally inconclusive items against the cumulative effect of another group of severally inconclusive items . . .'.[28] Elsewhere, Wisdom speaks of 'a move in thought which from a mass of data extracts and assembles what builds up into the proof of something which, though it doesn't go beyond the data, gives us an apprehension of reality which before we lacked'.[29] And in one of his legal examples already referrred to he describes the logic as 'a procedure in which we set this by that, and that by this, so as to see more plainly . . .'.[30] What Wisdom is getting at here is tolerably clear, but it raises the question of how the conclusion of such a non-experimental argument is related to what *is so*, to *fact*.

III.10   The precise question is now whether the defender (by Wisdomian logic and argument) of a non-experimental truth-claim comes into the possession of *factual knowledge* which hitherto he lacked. What Wisdom actually says about this is subtly ambiguous and requires the most careful interpretation. On the one hand, a first and casual reading of Wisdom might easily lead one to the conclusion that Wisdom tends to the view that this is not so, that *no factual difference whatever* is involved. If this were established, clearly the vast majority of theists would have enormous reservations about the value of his approach for metaphysical theology.[31] For example, the procedure of balancing the cumulative effect of one group of evidences against an opposite group is one which 'lends itself to description in terms of conflicting "probabilities",' and 'encourages the feeling that the issue is one of fact – that it is a matter of guessing from the premises at a further fact, at what is to come'. 'But this,' says Wisdom, 'is a muddle.' Rather the dispute is quite *a priori*. The 'unfactuality' of the conclusion is illustrated on several occasions by a medical example. For instance, we find him asserting that a non-experimental truth-question 'isn't a question like "has Jack diphtheria?" which can be settled by taking a swab from his throat'.[32] The logic he describes, that is, is not at all like that involved in a doctor guessing from a patient's symptoms what is wrong. This is so because the guesss may be confirmed or refuted by *further empirical observation*; he may be proved right or wrong by a subsequent X-ray or post-mortem examination. The basic reason, therefore, for Wisdom's unwillingness unambiguously to describe the conclusion of such disputes as 'factual' is the lack of *conceivable future empirical tests* either to prove or disprove it. This can be established from the parable itself: the two disputants in the garden are agreed that the gardener hypothesis 'is now not a matter of the one expecting something the other does not expect', i.e. *in the future*. Each of them defends his conclusion about the garden 'in spite of the fact that neither expects anything of it which the other does not expect', i.e. *in the future*. As we have seen, Wisdom refuses to encourage the feeling that it is 'all a matter of guessing from the premises at *a further fact, at*

what is to come' (italics mine). Nor is the issue at all like that
which faces a detective who 'from many clues guesses the
criminal', because here once more the guess may be confirmed
or refuted by *future empirical observations*. In other words, the logic
expounded by Wisdom here does not involve rational connections 'like those in inductions in which from many signs we guess
at *what is to come*' (italics mine). It is passages like these which
easily deceive the casual reader of Wisdom's writings on religion
into thinking that Wisdom's position is that the conclusions of
non-experimental disputes involve no reference to what is *in fact*
so, to how the world is. But this is not so.

III.11   To what *kind* of conclusions, then, do such arguments
lead? Finding the answer involves us in an examination of
Wisdom's terminology. For example, in the parable, one disputant says 'I *believe* that someone comes . . . I *believe* that the more
carefully we look the more we shall find confirmation of this'
(italics mine). Hence the conclusion is in the form of a reasoned
belief: a *belief that* the gardener comes, *that* God exists and acts,
and hence clearly *a belief that such-and-such is as a matter of fact the
case*. Again, Wisdom use the terminology of *giving a name* to a
situation or state of affairs: one disputant exclaims 'a garden!',
the other 'a wilderness!'; each disputant insists on the features of
the case which are 'in favour of calling the situation *by the name*
by which he wishes to call it' (italics mine). But, insists Wisdom,
the *belief* has a logic and rationality of its own, just as the application of a name is not merely the application of a name, just as
the pinning on of a medal is not merely the pinning on of a bit of
metal.[33] In court of a law, the application of a name (we think
of *Guilty!*, *Not Guilty!*) is the application of something in which 'a
game is lost and won and a game with very heavy stakes'.
Indeed, Wisdom insists, when the judge chooses such a name he
cannot do so without taking up an *attitude*, making a *declaration*,
making a *decision*, giving a *ruling*, and emitting an *exclamation*, all
of which involve a certain logic and rationality, a reasoned consideration of right and wrong, true and false. Hence, in Wisdom's view, the conclusion of such arguments lead us to 'an

apprehension of reality which before we lacked' (italics mine).[34] So far as theism is concerned, the logic of the exclamation 'divine!' is surprisingly like that involved in such exclamations as 'deplorable!', 'graceful!' and 'grand!'. Hence we must beware of the temptation to interpret Wisdom as saying that the conclusions of non-experimental arguments involve no reference as to what is factually so.

III.12   Indeed, Wisdom can on occasion state plainly that the issue *is*, in a sense, a *factual* one (though the passsages in which he does so must be read in the light of those in which he insists that such 'facts' are not actually or potentially observable). For example, Wisdom holds that those who dispute about belief in God quite properly 'speak as if they are concerned with a matter of . . . trans-sensual, trans-scientific and metaphysical fact, but still of fact and still a matter about which reasons for and against may be offered . . .'.[35] Elsewhere, he states plainly that '. . . *if we say . . . that when a difference as to the existence of a God is not one as to future happenings then it is not experimental and therefore not as to the facts, we must not forthwith assume that there is no right and wrong about it, nor . . . that the procedure is in no sense a discovery of new facts.'*[36] Wisdom's view of the factuality of the theistic conclusion comes out when, having conceded that there could not be a fool-proof proof of God, he continues in this way: 'But that doesn't mean that there are no evidences of God's existence; it doesn't mean that there are no proofs of his existence; nor that these are not to be found in experience; not even that they are not to be found in what we see and hear.'[37] It comes out even more strongly in a passage like the following:

> . . . we must insist that a person who in speaking of the gods expresses no belief as to what in fact is so is essentially different from one who does. Can we allow that his words still express what are in essence religious beliefs? Can we say that it is not of the essence of what we mean by a religious pronouncement that it should express some belief as to what the world is like? . . . I cannot here argue this question at length. But I believe the answer is No. It seems to me that *some belief as to what the world is like is of the essence of religion* (italics mine).[38]

In similar vein, Wisdom argues that the philosophical position which holds 'that it is not of the essence of religion to say something as to what in fact is so' may quite reasonably be met by the religious man with the accusation that this is 'a blasphemous fable and a dangerous deceit'. This is, argues Wisdom, because '. . . it tries to take from the doctrines of religion, not merely something without which they would not *strictly* speaking be religious, but something without which they would no longer be themselves.'[39]

III.13 The result of the enquiry that we opened up in III.10 is therefore that, on the basis of the evidence examined, Wisdom inclines strongly towards the view that the conclusions of non-experimental arguments about the nature of the world (formulated according to the logic which he describes) do indeed involve their defenders in claims to the possession of factual knowledge acquired by the use of these arguments, although it must be conceded that the facts involved are, in the nature of the case, not such as to lend themselves to actual or potential direct observation, nor to the construction of testable predictions about the future course of worldly events.

III.14 In III.6 we mentioned also certain *epistemological techniques* elucidated by Wisdom which may be used in order that persuasion may be undertaken and conclusions reached in non-experimental disputes. We turn now to an examination of these. The first of them is 'the Connecting Technique'.[40] The purpose of this is to reveal or prove beauty, to remove a blindness, to induce an attitude which is lacking, to reduce an attitude which is inappropriate. In using this technique the disputant re-concentrates attention on the overall picture which he finds significant, pointing up the presence and significance of this and that and this other aspect of it, *connecting* these up into an overall pattern in order to get his partner in dialogue to *see* things *as* he does. Something of this may be illustrated from the situation where the reader of a book marks certain passages with inks of different colours, so that the book, when read and marked, comes to exhibit certain rhythms, certain strands of argument based upon connected passages, certain patterns which the reader has found and to which he wishes to draw attention. Or it may be illustrated from the case of the author who cross-indexes his manuscript with the purpose of drawing attention to connections between apparently diverse and unconnected passages, connections which in his view give the work a pattern, an overall meaning or impact which might easily be missed. Or it may be illustrated from the parable itself, where one disputant says, in effect, 'Look at this arrangement here, look at that indication of purpose there, look at that instance of beauty over there. This *connects* with that and both *connect* with that over there.' The *connections* thus established become heuristic: in their light the disputant goes on looking and comes on new things which reinforce and extend the connections already made, so that a pattern of significance, of meaning, is gradually built up. His opponent does the opposite, builds up *connections* which for him form a pattern pointing to an opposite conclusion. In Wisdom's view, easily overlooked features of a picture or argument may be emphasized by placing beside them other pictures or arguments and by drawing illuminating connections between them. As an example of what Wisdom is getting at here Mr D. Z. Phillips points to the Old Testament narrative where Nathan the prophet illumined a certain pattern in the behaviour of King David by placing beside it a story about another pattern of behaviour, and by drawing connections between the two (II Sam. 12.1ff.).[41] The whole point of doing so, in Wisdom's view, is 'to remove a blindness, to induce an attitude which is lacking, and to reduce an attitude which is inappropriate'. A similar situation, according to Wisdom, may exist in the case where, when we regard the demented lover's love as gravely misplaced, we try to reason him out of it.[42] We do so by *connecting* up certain things done by his beloved into a pattern or by connecting things she has done with similar things done by others, things which have evoked from the lover disgust and fury. Of course, the technique may or may not work – the lover, despite all that we do, may continue to love.

III.15 The second technique is 'the Disconnecting Technique'. Here the attempt is made to persuade a disputant that he has been making connections that are unwarranted, and hence to persuade by *disconnecting*.[43] Sometimes such misconnections are made unconsciously. We can imagine one disputant in the garden saying, 'No, that does not really connect with this, and neither ought really to be connected up with this other.' We might say here that patterns or rhythms are being dismantled as a stage on the way to persuasion and conviction. Or we might say that patterns or rhythms are being dismantled in order that the superiority in scope and significance of an alternative pattern may be established.

III.16 There remains the question of what precisely Wisdom would claim to have established in his analysis of the logic involved in religious belief. Minimally, Wisdom would make the not insignificant claim that he had disposed of the positivist position that theological (and logically similar) issues are time-consuming nonsense, on the grounds that there are no conceivable experimental methods by which disagreements about them could be cleared up. His viewpoint here may be summarized in his own words: 'In these essays it is submitted that questions which neither observation and experiment nor yet further thought will settle may yet present real problems and even problems as to matter of fact. It is submitted that questions which "have no answers" may yet present problems which have solutions . . .'.[44] But what more than this could Wisdom claim to have established? Again, we may supply the answer in his own words: '. . . I am not trying to prove that God does exist but only to prove that it is wrong to say that there could be no proof that he does or that he does not.'[45] The standpoint of the present volume, to be developed in later chapters, is that while the metaphysical theologian could hardly use Wisdom's analysis as the sole and sufficient basis of a postanalytic natural theology, nevertheless he must concede that this analysis is a most suggestive description of *some ways in which the job might be tackled*, and of *how certain essential issues might be handled*.[46]

III.17 We continue our examination of 'seeing as' in practice by considering another parable whose author claims that it has been developed from Wisdom's. This is Antony Flew's parable which is to be found in the 'Theology and Falsification' section of *New Essays in Philosophical Theology*.[47] The relevant section of Flew's parable is as follows:

> Let us begin with a parable. It is a parable developed from a tale told by John Wisdom in his haunting and revelatory article 'Gods'. Once upon a time two explorers came upon a clearing in the jungle. In the clearing were growing many flowers and many weeds. One explorer says, 'Some gardener must tend this plot'. The other disagrees, 'There is no gardener'. So they pitch their tents and set a watch. No gardener is ever seen. 'But perhaps he is an invisible gardener.' So they set up a barbed-wire fence. They electrify it. They patrol with bloodhounds. (For they remember how H. G. Wells's *The Invisible Man* could be both smelt and touched though he could not be seen.) But no shrieks ever suggest that some intruder has received a shock. No movements of the wire ever betray an invisible climber. The bloodhounds never give cry. Yet still the Believer is not convinced. 'But there is a gardener, invisible, intangible, insensible to electric shocks, a gardener who has no scent and makes no sound, a gardener who comes secretly to look after the garden which he loves.' At last the Sceptic despairs, 'But what remains of your original assertion? Just how does what you call an invisible, intangible, eternally elusive gardener differ from an imaginary gardener or even from no gardener at all?'
>
> In this parable we can see how what starts as an assertion, that something exists or that there is an analogy between certain complexes of phenomena, may be reduced step by step to an altogether different status, to an expression perhaps of a 'picture preference'. The Sceptic says there is no gardener. The Believer says there is a gardener (but invisible, etc.). One man talks about sexual behaviour. Another man prefers to talk of Aphrodite (but knows that there is not really a superhuman person additional to, and somehow responsible for, all sexual phenomena). The process of qualification may be checked at any point before the original assertion is completely withdrawn and something of that first assertion will remain (Tautology). Mr Wells's invisible man could not, admittedly, be seen, but in all other respects he was a man like the rest of us. But though the process of qualification may be, and of course usually is, checked in time, it is not always judiciously so halted. Someone may dissipate his assertion completely without noticing that he had done so. A fine brash hypothesis may thus be killed by inches, the death by a thousand qualifications.

III.18 There is one fact, an unfortunate one perhaps, which must be carefully noted. It is that Flew's parable, and the conclusions drawn from it, are probably very much better known and have been more widely discussed in Anglo-American circles than are Wisdom's. Hence there is the widespread but mistaken impression that Flew has been a trenchant popularizer of Wisdom and that Flew's parable is but a more incisive version of Wisdom's. But this is not so. Although he does not mention Flew by name, there can be little doubt that D. Z. Phillips has him in mind when he writes of Wisdom's philosophy of religion:

> Wisdom is saying, then, that although in one sense all the facts may be known in another sense questions involving a greater apprehension of the facts may remain. Many philosophers of religion have ignored this aspect of Wisdom's work. They have been content to conclude that since religious beliefs are not experimental hypotheses, they cannot tell us anything about what is so, about what is in fact the case. They have ignored the arguments Wisdom provides to show conclusively that this conclusion suffers from too narrow a conception of what is so and of what constitutes 'the facts'. Nor have philosophers been slow to use some of Wisdom's observations, for example, his parable of the long-neglected garden, to support their conclusions, despite the fact that taken in context these observations serve merely as the prelude to Wisdom's positive contributions to the determination of the logic of religious beliefs. As a result, Wisdom's philosophy of religion remains, at best, half-discussed.[48]

And Mr Renford Bambrough, again not mentioning Flew by name, points out 'that Wisdom's treatment, which is offered as a neutral account of the logic of theological disputes, has found more favour among atheists and agnostics than among their theological opponents. ...'[49] We must therefore raise the question as to the purpose and achievement of Flew as compared with those of Wisdom.

III.19 One significant difference between the work of Wisdom here and that of Flew in that *in the total context of Wisdom's writings on religion* the parable of the garden does not matter all that much, or even that Wisdom's positive contribution to the philosophy of religion would stand if Wisdom *had omitted the parable* altogether, making the points vividly communicated by the parable in more abstract terminology. (In this context, Phillips's remarks above about '*some* of Wisdom's observations', and 'the parable ... *taken in context*', and the parable 'as the *prelude* to ...' are very much to the point.) Indeed, if Wisdom's account of religious belief were communicated to us only by Flew's parable and its context,[50] Wisdom's account of religious belief would remain very much less than 'half-discussed'. Wisdom's reason for composing the little tale (a small proportion of the totality of his writings having a bearing on religious belief) is to indicate, parabolically and symbolically (and therefore in a way open to misinterpretation), *the sort of thing involved in seeing the world as one thing or another*. But it would be difficult to argue that Wisdom's total account of the logic of religious belief stands or falls by the satisfactoriness of the tale of the garden.

III.20 We can put the same thing in another way: in Wisdom's total work having a bearing on religion there is to be found a mass of diverse problems and situations through which he attempts to articulate the logic involved in deciding about non-experimental truth-claims, religious, legal, commercial, medical, aesthetic, existential and psychoanalytic ones; within this mass there is the parable of the garden. Flew extracts the parable from this context and proceeds to demonstrate one set of inferences that can be drawn from it, and ignores other and in many instances much more complex ones, and the logic which, in Wisdom's view, they generate. Hence the limitation of his discussion. But given this limitation, Flew's discussion does point up very clearly several crucial issues which Wisdom's use of the parable ought to bring to our attention.

III.21 One of these is the problem of the curious limitation of the premises of the argument developed from the parable – namely, the apparent *limitation* of the premises of a theistic demonstration to *order and disorder in the natural world*. In Wisdom's parable, one set of evidences within the garden consists of arrangement, beauty, purpose, order and the like, while the opposing set consists of weeds, disorder, purposelessness and the like. Similarly, in Flew's parable the opposing sets consist of tended flowers and haphazard weeds. Hence, if the parables are taken literally as what is involved in seeing the world *as* something or other, we limit our premises to those of the eighteenth-century form of the teleological argument. And occasionally

Wisdom does display a certain preoccupation with premises of a similar kind. For instance, in 'The Logic of God' we read that '. . . the evidences of his (i.e. God's) existence lie in the order and arrangement of nature', and that 'I understand that you are now saying that the order and arrangement of nature proves the existence of God'.[51] (We find the same sort of thing, as we might expect, in an empiricist like Ayer: 'It is sometimes claimed, indeed, that the existence of a certain sort of regularity in nature constitutes sufficient evidence for the existence of a god.'[52]) One of the damning limitations of many Anglo-Saxon discussions of the divine existence is the sometimes obsessive concentration of attention upon order and regularity in nature as premises for theistic demonstration. Damning, because the ensuing argument is at once opened up to the lethal criticisms of this type of argument accumulated by empiricists from the publication of Hume's *Dialogues* until the present day. Now Flew is a distinguished Humean scholar, and one of the things implied by Hare's phrase (III.19[50] above) 'on the grounds marked out by Flew' is Flew's significant limitation of theistic premises to those of *natural order and regularity*, a type of demonstration notoriously and devastatingly vulnerable to Humean scepticism. While we must in all fairness keep in mind that elsewhere than in the parable Wisdom is guilty of no such limitation, this issue should bring home to us forcibly that in any attempt to develop a natural theology from the notion of 'seeing as' the premises must be much wider and more heterogeneous than those of any physico-theological argument.

III.22 Nevertheless, Flew's parable possesses great merit. Commenting upon *New Essays in Philosophical Theology*, Wisdom remarks of Flew's contribution that it 'presents clearly yet sympathetically the difficulty he finds in what is said by men of religion'.[53] For Flew has put his finger firmly upon one of the crucial issues in discourse about God. The Being talked about by the religious believer, Flew emphasizes, is qualitatively uniquely odd, in that he is invisible, intangible, insensitive to physical stimuli, odourless, soundless and empirically very elusive indeed. Now what *kind* of Being is this, he is asking? How does he differ from a sheer fiction, or from no Being at all? Does it make any sense to talk of a Being who so completely transcends the everyday spatio-temporal world and so elusively slips through every gap in the mesh of its truth-claim tests? What Flew is getting at is, in the last analysis, that one would require very very strong grounds indeed before one were forced into the position of assenting to the existence of such a Being. To leap from 'certain complexes of phenomena' or from a certain 'world-picture' to the existence of such a non-empirical Being is to make such a staggeringly huge leap that Flew believes it to be more reasonable to remain with one's feet firmly on the ground – to remain at the level of a 'picture preference' or of the apprehension of some 'analogy between certain complexes of phenomena'. For, according to Flew, the trouble with theistic beliefs and utterances is their relationship with the *facts*: the man who utters theistic assertions has before him *a mass of facts*; the man who denies them has before him the same mass of facts. What *difference* is there between them? Why does one make the terrific leap beyond the facts that he does? For to assert something factual is presumably to deny something factual; to deny something factual is presumably to make some factual assertion or other. How can this be so if theistic assertions apparently do not deny one or more factual assertions, since (at the level of experience, perception, etc.) there is apparently no *factual* difference between theist and non-theist? Are theistic assertions therefore assertions at all? Or are they pseudo-assertions, possessing the correct grammatical but the incorrect logical form possessed by all assertions? The points here thrown up by Flew's discussion are very important and something tentative must be said about them before we go further.

III.23 What, then, is the relationship between theistic propositions and *facts*? What *facts*, how many *facts*, what series of *facts*, could negate them? The difficulty here is that, as we have seen, *what* the facts *are* is not at all self-evident. It is just not true to say, as was said above, that when the theist makes an assertion and the non-theist denies it, each has *the same mass of facts* before him. It is to Wisdom's great credit that he has shown from a heterogeneous mass of situations that sharp differences arise out of the ways in which facts may be grouped, patterned, structured, connected together, and the like; these differences spring from rational attempts to attain to a 'greater apprehension' of the facts. If so, the simple phrase 'mass of facts' will not do, on Kantian as on Wisdomian grounds. For the facts are not simply seen, but 'seen as'. Now if the theist is, as we have been arguing, one whose belief (from the standpoint of reason) is reached by or based upon 'seeing the entire world as a sacred place', and if this vision of the world is used by him heuristically (III.3), it follows that as further factual events occur (or as facts belonging to the past are brought to his attention) they must be *related to his heuristic picture of the world as a whole*. How is this done? On the one hand, certain types of fact might appear to corroborate his picture and might click into place with the facility of the missing jigsaw-piece. On the other, certain types might fit only very irregularly or awkwardly, or even be so inappropriately shaped that the only reasonable course would be to acknowledge this inappropriateness, and concede that its existence counts as evidence against the convincingness of the picture as a whole. It is indeed reasonable to ask whether such a theist would be willing, having had overlooked or neglected facts brought to his attention, to abandon his picture of the world altogether? On Wisdomian grounds, the answer would be Yes. According to Wisdom's neutralist description of the logic of religious belief, one disputant may indeed, by argument, by connecting and disconnecting, by accumulating factual evidences which 'severally co-operate in favour of a certain conclusion', bring his opponent to see that the facts *as a structured whole* are not what hitherto he had taken them to be, and hence to abandon the picture of the world which hitherto he held. Wisdomian techniques are available to theist and naturalist alike. But this need not happen. For his part, the theist might on reflection argue that a *prima facie* inappropriate fact (such as the fact of suffering or evil) can appropriately be fitted into his overall perspective. Indeed, one important section of classical metaphysical theology, *theodicy*, has always aimed at relating suffering and evil significantly to the wider vision of the world as derived from and dependent upon an infinitely benevolent deity.[54]

III.24 We may apply this analysis to the concrete problem used by Flew to make his point.[55] This is the case of the father whose child lies dying of inoperable cancer, and who is told that nevertheless 'God loves us', loves us as a father loves his children. In the apparent absence of empirical divine aid, the original assertion is qualified – the love in question is 'not merely human', or it is 'inscrutable', or something of the kind. Flew enquires about just what would have to happen to produce the situation where the original assertion ('God loves us') is quite eroded away by the facts, and is abandoned altogether. If what we have been saying in preceding paragraphs makes sense, the answer to Flew's inquiry would take this form: *It all depends upon the structure of the original belief in God.* (Of course, the belief may not have been reached by any *a posteriori* route at all; it may be quite *a priori*, or based upon some transcendental, overwhelming and incorrigible revelation which no amount of factual evidence could apparently undermine.) But if the belief in question is empirical, if it is significantly related to a complex of facts, the question of its erosion concerns the relation of the overlooked or unconsidered awkward fact to belief considered as a heuristic vision or picture of the world as a whole, or as a reasonably structured synopsis of *all* one's experience. Is the weight and character of this fact such that it can significantly be fitted into the picture, or that it can be fitted in only with great difficulty, or that the picture must now be completely dismantled or abandoned? If this latter course is taken, this may be because the 'belief' in question was originally little more than unexamined wishful thinking; that is, not a genuine empirical belief at all. Or it may be because the belief in question was too narrowly based, being little more perhaps than a naïf calculation that pleasure-states vastly outnumber quantitatively and are more intense qualitatively than suffering-states. At any rate, in general the answer to Flew's inquiry is that the occurrence of fresh facts, or the contemplation of overlooked facts, may indeed make a difference to religious belief. And if Flew presses the point and enquires if there is any conceivable state of affairs whose actualization would require us to abandon the picture altogether, the theoretical answer must be that, if religious beliefs are truly empirical, this is indeed so. 'Could anything count decisively against . . . the assertion that God is merciful? Yes, suffering which was utterly, eternally and irredeemably pointless.'[56] This is a matter to which we must return below.

III.25 To return briefly to Flew's question 'Just how does what you call an invisible, intangible, eternally elusive gardener differ from an imaginary gardener or even from no gardener at all?', there is another answer worth mentioning briefly at this stage. If this question may fairly be reformulated as 'What *difference* does all this talk of the gardener make in the last analysis?', one significant answer is that theistic belief, once acquired, makes a huge difference to how man regards his world and his relation to it, to those ways in which he relates himself to his environment, to what he can hope for, to his intercourse with his fellows, to how he interprets much that is problematic in his life. It matters little to an observer whether he sees a Wittgensteinian puzzle-picture as a duck or as a rabbit, but it *matters* immeasurably to a participant whether the world is seen as a theistic rather than as an atheistic place. R. M. Hare hints at this kind of thing in this way:

> Suppose we believed that everything that happened, happened by pure chance. This would not of course be an assertion; for it is compatible with anything happening or not happening, and so, incidentally, is it contradictory. But if we had this belief, we should not be able to explain or predict or plan anything. Thus, although we should not be *asserting* anything different from those of a more normal belief, there would be a great difference between us; and this is the sort of difference between those who believe in God and those who really disbelieve in him.[57]

In other words, theistic beliefs and utterances (like, as we shall

argue below, many metaphysical ones) are partly anthropological or existential ones.

III.26 Another merit of Flew's paper, already touched upon, is
that it raises with uncompromising sharpness the question of the
counter-evidence for theism. Above we spoke, rather optimistically perhaps, of the natural theologian fitting awkward or
inappropriate facts into a theistic picture of the world, and of
relating suffering and evil significantly to a wider vision of the
world (III.23, 24). But is it enough to say this? What precisely
do we mean, for example, by 'significantly'? How can facts of
suffering or evil be 'fitted into' a vision of the world as derived
from and dependent upon an infinitely benevolent creator? It is
to Flew's great credit that he made theologians raise and answer
such questions afresh. We shall explore them further in our next
chapter.

NOTES

1. Part II, xi, pp. 193^{ef}.
2. P. 194^e.
3. P. 195^e.
4. *Ibid.*
5. *Ibid.*
6. *Ibid.*, p. 196^e.
7. P. 197^e.
8. *Ibid.*
9. P. 200^e.
10. P. 198^e.
11. Cf. the definition of natural theology in I.2 above.
12. These terms are used in the discussion in H. D. Lewis, *Philosophy of
Religion*, London, 1965, pp. 99f.
13. The paper is reprinted in full in *Proc. Arist. Soc.*, 1944–5, *Logic and
Language* I, ed. Antony Flew, Oxford, 1951, Wisdom's *Philosophy and Psycho-
analysis*, Oxford, 1953, and in *Classical and Contemporary Readings in the
Philosophy of Religion*, ed. John Hick, Englewood Cliffs, N.J., 1964: it has been
partially reprinted in *Philosophy of Religion: A Book of Readings*, eds. G. L.
Abernethy and T. A. Langford, Second Edition, New York, 1968; Wisdom's
parable has been reprinted in *A Reader in Contemporary Theology*, eds. J.
Bowden and J. Richmond, London and Philadelphia, 1967, pp. 146–8.
Page-references given below are to the text of *Logic and Language* I.
References will also be made to two of Wisdom's papers, 'The Logic of God',
and 'Religious Belief', in *Paradox and Discovery*, Oxford, 1965.

14. *Logic and Language* I, pp. 192–3.

15. *Ibid.*, p. 187.

16. But see III.9f. below.

17. 'The Logic of God', in *Paradox and Discovery*, p. 8: cf. 'We all know and, what is more, we all recognize that there are questions which though they don't call for further investigation but only for reflection are yet perfectly respectable because the reflection they call for may be carried out in a definite demonstrative procedure which gives results Yes or No', *op. cit.*, p. 6.

18. *Ibid.*, p. 7.

19. *Ibid.*, pp. 7–8.

20. *Logic and Language*, p. 195.

21. *Ibid.*, p. 196.

22. *Paradox and Discovery*, p. 7.

23. *Ibid.*

24. *Ibid.*, p. 21.

25. *Ibid.*, p. 55.

26. *Logic and Language*, p. 197.

27. *Ibid.*, p. 196; elsewhere, Wisdom asserts that the logic this kind of question calls for 'cannot be conducted by a definite step-by-step procedure like that of one who calculates the height or weight or prospects of life of the average man . . .', *Paradox and Discovery*, p. 22.

28. *Logic and Language*, p. 195.

29. *Paradox and Discovery*, p. 13.

30. *Ibid.*, p. 55.

31. For what follows, see *Logic and Language*, pp. 195–7.

32. *Paradox and Discovery*, p. 9.

33. *Logic and Language*, p. 196.

34. *Paradox and Discovery*, p. 13.

35. *Logic and Language*, p. 194.

36. *Ibid.*, p. 197.

37. *Paradox and Discovery*, p. 12.

38. *Ibid.*, pp. 53–4.

39. *Ibid.*, p. 55.

40. *Logic and Language*, p. 197.

41. D. Z. Phillips, 'Wisdom's Gods', *The Philosophical Quarterly*, vol. 19, no. 74, January, 1969, p. 21.

42. *Logic and Language*, pp. 198–9.

43. *Ibid.*, pp. 199–201.

44. *Paradox and Discovery*, Introduction.

45. *Ibid.*, p. 14.

46. For exposition and criticism of Wisdom's account of the logic of religious belief, see D. Z. Phillips, 'Wisdom's Gods', and Renford Bambrough, *Reason, Truth and God*, London, 1969, esp. chapter 4, 'Patterns', pp. 55–72.

47. Eds. Antony Flew and Alasdair MacIntyre, London, 1955, pp. 96f.

48. 'Wisdom's Gods', p. 19.

49. *Reason, Truth and God*, p. 65.

50. 'I must begin by confessing that, *on the ground marked out by Flew*, he

seems to me to be completely victorious', R. M. Hare, *New Essays in Philosophical Theology*, p. 99 (italics mine).

51. *Paradox and Discovery*, pp. 11 and 13.

52. *Language, Truth and Logic*, p. 115.

53. *Paradox and Discovery*, p. 43.

54. According to Karl Rahner, theodicy '. . . signifies the . . . demonstration by philosophical or Christian reasoning that evil in the world (suffering, misfortune, death, sin) in the biological and human spheres does not preclude philosophical or religious belief in the existence of a holy God who is infinitely perfect and good', *Concise Theological Dictionary*, p. 454. See John Hick, *Evil and the God of Love*, London, 1966, and *God and Evil*, ed. Nelson Pike, Englewood Cliffs, N.J., 1964.

55. *New Essays in Philosophical Theology*, pp. 98–9.

56. I. M. Crombie, in *New Essays in Philosophical Theology*, p. 124; but Crombie goes on to show that it would be extremely difficult to say precisely what such suffering would be like.

57. *New Essays*, pp. 101–2; Hare goes on to deplore the detachment of the explorers in Flew's parable. They do not *mind about*, they are not *concerned with* the garden. But in other types of parable, as we shall see, the characters are participants in something about which they are deeply concerned.

IV

PARABLES, PATTERNS AND PERSPECTIVES

IV.1 We resume our examination of 'seeing as' in practice by considering yet one more parable, one which was generated in response to the conclusions which Flew drew from his. Its author is Basil Mitchell, and it is to be found, like Flew's, in the 'Theology and Falsification' section of *New Essays in Philosophical Theology*.[1] The text of the parable is as follows:

> In time of war in an occupied country, a member of the resistance meets one night a stranger who deeply impresses him. They spend that night together in conversation. The Stranger tells the partisan that he himself is on the side of the resistance – indeed that he is in command of it, and urges the partisan to have faith in him no matter what happens. The partisan is utterly convinced at that meeting of the Stranger's sincerity and constancy and undertakes to trust him.
>
> They never meet in conditions of intimacy again. But sometimes the Stranger is seen helping members of the resistance, and the partisan is grateful and says to his friends, 'He is on our side'.
>
> Sometimes he is seen in the uniform of the police handing over patriots to the occupying power. On these occasions his friends murmur against him: but the partisan still says, 'He is on our side'. He still believes that, in spite of appearances, the Stranger did not deceive him. Sometimes he asks the Stranger for help and receives it. He is then thankful. Sometimes he asks and does not receive it. Then he says, 'The Stranger knows best'. Sometimes his friends, in exasperation, say 'Well, what *would* he have to do for you to admit that you were wrong and that he is not on our side?' But the partisan refuses to answer. He will not consent to put the Stranger to the test. And sometimes his friends complain, 'Well, if *that's* what you mean by his being on our side, the sooner he goes over to the other side the better.'
>
> The partisan of the parable does not allow anything to count decisively against the proposition 'The Stranger is on our side'. This is because he has committed himself to trust the Stranger. But he of course recognizes that the Stranger's ambiguous behaviour *does* count against what he believes about him. It is precisely this situation which constitutes the trial of his faith.

IV.2 At first sight, this parable possesses characteristics with which we are already familiar from our examination of those of Wisdom and Flew. There is the same description of a puzzling or problematic situation within which experimental testing is out of the question, there is the same *ambiguity* running through the evidence, there are the two opposed disputants (or groups of disputants) in disagreement about the correct interpretation to be put on a total factual state of affairs, about what a 'greater apprehension' of the facts involves. Yet there are also crucial dissimilarities which must be carefully explored.

IV.3 One striking dissimilarity is that we are no longer in a country garden or in a flower-bedecked clearing in a jungle, but in a country torn by war, in a battlefield. Moreover, we no longer have two detached visitors to a garden, but participants, actors, agents, involved in a desperate and dangerous situation. And the decision involved is no longer a detached, theoretical, academic one about the causes of flower-beds falling into partial disorder, but one with a desperate existential urgency attached to it, a life-or-death decision, as we might say. To use fashionable Heideggerian terminology, the participants experience their *thrownness*; they are *thrown* willy-nilly into existence at an apparently fortuitous point; they have no choice in the matter. They are therefore obliged to plot and chart their position within the total situation. They must map out their position *vis-à-vis* the enemy, each other, the Stranger, ambiguous items of evidence, and so on. This dissimilarity is a significant one (III.25).

IV.4 Another striking dissimilarity is the place given in this parable to *trust* and *faith*. This point links up with the questions we raised in III.26, about how facts of suffering and evil can be significantly related to a theistic vision of the world. The answer to these suggested by Mitchell's parable is that the first two parables examined are defective in overlooking the essential element of *trust* involved in the man–God relation. What can this possibly mean for a metaphysical theology? If it means anything at all, it must mean that within the overall theistic picture

of the world, facts of evil, suffering and apparent meaningless-
ness have the *positive and significant function* of ensuring that man's
response to God within the world is not forced from him, but is
free from coercion from without. Man is therefore free to trust or
not to trust: the awkward and inappropriate facts allow him not
to trust. The beneficence of God within the world is not forced
overwhelmingly upon man, it is not unambiguously self-evident,
but is balanced by counter-evidence. Why is this important?
The only answer at this stage is that if we are discussing theism
of a Hebrew-Christian type, an utterly essential ingredient of
such theism is that the relation between man and God should
be analogously similar to relations of unforced love, trust and
response in the sphere of relations between finite personal beings.
And such love and trust in this sphere would cease to be so if the
option of not loving and trusting were not a live one; one can
only freely commit oneself to 'trust' if occasionally circumstances
are such that one goes on trusting *despite* the presence of awkward
or inappropriate facts. One goes on trusting 'nevertheless, in
spite of. . . .'. The *function* of awkward facts is to test one's trust,
call it in question, and in the process develop and strengthen it.

IV.5 Yet another dissimilarity need only detain us briefly. It is
that the data over which the disagreement occurs are much more
complex and sophisticated than the data contained in the first
two parables. The kind of data appealed to by the defender of
the argument from design (natural order, regularity, and the
like) are left far behind. The appearance of the stranger, the
conversation, the demand for trust, the eliciting of faith, the
demands for help and the ambiguous responses to these – all of
these add up to a *complexity of data* lacking in the parables of
Wisdom and Flew. It could be argued indeed that the original
appearance of the stranger and his demand for trust in the midst of
occasionally adverse circumstances (a summary of the history
of the Incarnation) is a claim that *history* forms an essential part
of the data which enables the Christian to *see* the world *as* a holy
place. This links up with our earlier insistence that if Humean
scepticism is to be avoided the premises of any natural theology

developed from the notion of 'seeing as' must be much wider and heterogeneous than those of any physico-theological argument.

IV.6 The final dissimilarity worth noting is that there is in Mitchell's story a certain *movement, development* or *dynamism* lacking in the first two. For a war, after all, is something that has a beginning and an end. And when the war ends, there is in principle at any rate the possibility that the problem of the exact status of the stranger may be cleared up, when the post-war confusion has been tackled. But if so, this means that experimental verification of some kind (*pace* Wisdom!) cannot be completely ruled out of court. The theological reference here is to verification of religious beliefs after death. This point must be mentioned, if only because there are those who insist that theism of a Hebrew-Christian type cannot properly be discussed in isolation from this eschatological reference. Mr Ian Crombie, for example, while discussing the issue of the meaning and verification of religious beliefs, observes that the Christian significantly 'looks for the resurrection of the dead, and the life of the world to come; he believes, that is, that we do not see all of the picture, and that the parts which we do not see are precisely the parts which determine the design of the whole.'[2]

IV.7 From the parable, rightly interpreted, issues Mitchell's response to Flew's challenge. Factual events do make a *difference* to religious beliefs: the partisan 'recognizes that the stranger's ambiguous behaviour *does* count against what he believes about him'; hence his faith is put under strain, it is tried and tested. His commitment is called in question and must be re-examined in the light of the facts. This is enough to show that his vision of reality is no merely uncritical, psychogenic palliative. Yet the commitment is such that it is not abandoned each time an ambiguous or awkward fact has to be accounted for.

IV.8 We turn now to examine another parable, whose author is John Hick, which belongs, broadly speaking, to the same context in modern philosophical theology as those already examined, namely, the context of 'seeing as' as a response to the challenge of Anglo-Saxon empiricism. The text[3] of the parable is as follows:

> Two men are travelling together along a road. One of them believes that
> it leads to a Celestial City, the other that it leads nowhere; but since this is
> the only road there is, both must travel it. Neither has been this way
> before, and therefore neither is able to say what they will find around
> each corner. During their journey they meet both with moments of
> refreshment and delight, and with moments of hardship and danger. All
> the time one of them thinks of his journey as a pilgrimage to the Celestial
> City and interprets the pleasant parts as encouragements and the obstacles
> as trials of his purpose and lessons in endurance, prepared by the king of
> that city and designed to make of him a worthy citizen of the place when
> at last he arrives there. The other, however, believes none of this and sees
> his journey as an unavoidable and aimless ramble. Since he has no choice
> in the matter he enjoys the good and endures the bad. But for him there is
> no Celestial City to be reached, no all-encompassing purpose ordaining
> their journey – only the road itself and the luck of the road in good
> weather and in bad.
>   During the course of the journey the issue between them is not an
> experimental one. They do not entertain different expectations about the
> coming details of the road, but only about its ultimate destination. And
> yet when they do turn the last corner it will be apparent that one of them
> has been right all the time and the other wrong. Thus although the issue
> between them has not been experimental, it has nevertheless from the
> start been a real issue. They have not merely felt differently about the
> road; for one was feeling appropriately and the other inappropriately in
> relation to the actual state of affairs. Their opposed interpretations of the
> road constituted genuinely rival assertions, though assertions whose status
> has the peculiar characteristic of being guaranteed by a future crux.

IV.9 With this parable we are once more on ground that should
not be too unfamiliar to us (cf. IV.2–7 above). We have once
again a puzzling state of affairs which cannot be tackled experimentally; there is the evidence characterized strongly by
ambiguity, the two disputants in sharp disagreement about the
correct *interpretation* of the total factual complex; as in Mitchell's
parable, we see once more the *thrownness* of the disputants who
try to *map out* their exact location in relation to the road, the
weather, favourable and adverse circumstances, and the alleged
destination; as we shall note below, there is a strong emphasis on
trust; the obstacles, the hardship and the danger *function positively* to test the faith and mature the character of the traveller;
once more also, the data, the evidence, appealed to are much
more *complex* than those of any argument from natural design;

and in Hick's parable the notion of *development* or *movement* comes out very strongly within the context of the journey from point of departure to destination. Finally, the *eschatological* reference in Hick is more explicit than implicit. But one similarity between the parable of Hick and that of Wisdom is that it can only be fully understood if it is looked at within the context of a wider contribution to the contemporary epistemology of religion. We now turn to consider several significant points from this contribution.

IV.10 We have spoken above of *interpretation*, and it is interpretation which has already been implicitly at least a crucial issue in our discussions of Wisdom, Flew and Mitchell; indeed it was a concept which we encountered within Wittgenstein's account of 'seeing as'.[4] In Hick, religious faith is described as the 'interpretative' element within religious experience, by means of which 'significance' is found within reality. All knowledge is consciousness of significance; it is significance which builds up for us a stable and ordered world, rather than an 'empty void', a 'churning chaos' or a sheer 'buzzing, booming confusion'.[5] Correlated with significance is *interpretation*, a term which 'suggests the possibility of differing judgments; we tend to call a conclusion an interpretation when we recognize that there may be other and variant accounts of the same subject matter'.[6] The terms 'significance' and 'interpretation' both point to a 'suggestion of ambiguity in the given'.[7] The connection between these terms and our earlier discussions is apparent. For it is not only isolated objects that can have significance for us, but also 'groups of objects standing in recognizable patterns of relations to one another'.[8] This can appropriately be called 'situational significance'. Nor can the objects thus grouped be confined to material ones; non-material entities (sounds, lights, emotions, attitudes) also enter into the groupings.[9] Moreover, Hick insists that 'significance is essentially related to action'[10] (we remember how Mitchell's partisan arrived at an *interpretation* of the stranger's significance which guided his *behaviour* within the resistance organization).

IV.11 'A "situation",' in Hick's view, 'may be defined . . . as a state of affairs which, when selected for attention by an act of interpretation, carries its own distinctive practical significance for us.'[11] Hick's thesis is that 'We may be involved in many different situations at the same time' and that 'there may thus occur an indefinitely complex interpenetration of situations.'[12] He contends that situational significance can be divided into three orders, those of nature, man and God, the second superimposed upon and presupposing the first, and the third superimposed upon and presupposing the first two.[13] The relationships between the three may also be described in terms of *interpenetration*.

IV.12 Our perception of the lowest of the three orders, that of nature, our everyday environment, involves us in *interpretation*. Even in relation to the natural world, 'the perceiving mind is . . . always in some degree a selecting, relating and synthesizing agent, and experiencing our environment involves a continuous activity of interpretation' (although such 'interpretation' is an unconscious and habitual process).[14] Such interpretation carries us 'into an objective world of enduring, causally interacting objects, which we share with other people'.[15] Such interpretation, such a mapping out of our natural environment, enables us to plan, to predict and to integrate our actions and policies with the laws of the material world.

IV.13 But man lives not only in relation to the natural world, but also as a person in relation with other persons. This fact leads Hick to say: 'And so we find that presupposing consciousness of the physical world, and supervening upon it, is the kind of situational significance which we call "being responsible" or "being under obligation".'[16] We might say that above the natural order there is a higher, moral order *superimposed upon* and *interpenetrating* the lower one. In Hick's writings we can find several concrete examples of what is meant here. In one of them an empirical state of affairs within the natural order is described – 'a particular configuration of stone and earth and flesh' – an injured stranger lying on an unfrequented road in need of help[17]. But an act of *moral* interpretation mediates to the traveller that he is in a situation of personal responsibility, that a demand for help is laid upon him. Elsewhere, Hick describes a different empirical state of affairs within the natural order – someone caught at the foot of a cliff by an incoming tide, crying for help. At the level of natural significance, we have 'the cliff and the sea, a human creature liable in due course to be submerged by the rising tide, and his shouted appeals for help'.[18] However, personal and moral beings are aware of *more than* a purely natural configuration – we can 'also experience them as constituting a situation of moral claim upon ourselves.'[19] Hick continues: 'The ethical is experienced as an order of significance which supervenes upon, interpenetrates, and is mediated through the physical significance which it presupposes.'[20] Hick rightly makes the point that the moral dimension of the situation may not be immediately apparent; it may take time for it to dawn upon us. When it does so, something happens which Hick interestingly links up with 'seeing as'. Something happens here 'that is comparable to the discovery of an emergent pattern in a puzzle picture'.

> As the same lines and marks are there, but we have now come to see them as constituting an importantly new pattern, so the social situation is there with the same describable features, but we have now come to be aware of it as laying upon us an inescapable moral claim.[21]

In the moral as in the purely natural situation an act of *interpretation* is involved. But at the moral level 'the interpretation is a more truly voluntary one' than in the natural. This is so because 'it is not forced upon us from outside, but depends upon an inner capacity and tendency to interpret in this way, a tendency which we are free to oppose and even to overrule'.[22]

IV.14 Superimposed upon, intervening upon, presupposing and interpenetrating the natural and moral orders is, in Hick's view, a third, the level of theistic religion, in which man is related to the divine order. This 'is a higher level of significance, adding a new dimension which both includes and transcends that of moral judgment, and yet on the other hand it does not form a simple continuation of the pattern we have already noted'.[23] Its complexity can be indicated thus: 'Not every moment of religious awareness is superimposed upon some occasion of moral obligation.' But often 'the sense of the presence of God does carry with it some specific or general moral demand'. On the other hand, the sense of God's presence does not always require a specific environmental context: for example, it may occur within the context of prayer, meditation and contemplation. Nor does it necessarily require the presence of another human being; it can occur in solitude, it may be mediated to us by the splendours of nature.[24] Theistic and ethical interpretation are akin in that the former 'is clearly focused in some situations and imperceptible in others'.[25] Although the believer may not be continuously conscious of God's presence, yet the point is reached where he is 'conscious rather of the divine will as a reality in the background of his life, a reality which may at any time emerge to confront him in absolute and inescapable demand'.[26] The sphere in which this is accomplished 'is not merely this or that isolable situation, but the uniquely total situation constituted by our experience as a whole and in all its aspects, up to the present moment'.[27] In several places Hick applies his notion of faith as 'experiencing-as' to the biblical records of the Old and New Testaments.[28]

> In the prophetic interpretation of history embodied in the Old Testament records, events which would be described by a secular historian as the outcome of political, economic, sociological and geographical factors are *seen as* incidents in a dialogue which continues through the centuries between God and his people.[29]

IV.15 Hick's contribution to the epistemology of religion cannot be appreciated without some grasp of what he calls *cognitive freedom*. The crucial point is that the knowledge of God 'is not given to us as a compulsory perception, but is achieved as a voluntary act of interpretation'.[30] As human beings we are endowed with a measure of 'cognitive freedom'.[31] In coming to know we must often 'exert ourselves'. Knowing must often involve conscious choice, the will to know. Cognitive freedom,

clearly, 'is at a minimum in sense perception'.[32] Hence, its
operation is often overlooked, with the consequence that 'knowledge of the physical world has always been regarded by common sense as the standard type of knowledge, and . . . in our
contemporary Atlantic culture, the physical sciences are accor-
ded a unique authority as arbiters of truth'.[33] But it is quite
otherwise when we move upwards, so to speak, to the order of
morals and aesthetics; here 'variations and divergences of interpretation are at once apparent'.[34] Our capacity to appreciate
beauty is something that we can will to develop or neglect; to
get the most out of the aesthetic side of things we have to make
an effort, to 'go out of our way'.[35] It is not otherwise in the area
of moral experience. This is most clearly perceived in connection
with the phenomenon of 'moral blindness'. For, Hick argues,
human wrong-doing most frequently takes the form, not of
blatantly doing that which we clearly see to be wrong, but of
'turning . . . a blind eye to the moral facts of the situation', of
refusing 'to see our neighbour's need as constituting a call upon
ourselves'.[36] Thus, 'wilful moral blindness is an exercise of
cognitive freedom'.[37]

IV.16 Cognitive freedom, Hick goes on to argue, is 'at a
maximum . . . in our cognition of the religious significance of
our environment, its significance as mediating the divine presence'.[38] Here Hick utilizes Buber's distinction between I-Thou
and I-It relationships to make his point. The analysis of the
I-Thou relationship, in Hick's view, has brought home strongly
to us that 'In all fully personal dealings with people we respect
their personal independence and integrity; . . . we regard them
as of the same ultimate status as ourselves, so that their views
and wishes, their hopes and fears, their arguments and prejudices,
are entitled to consideration along with our own.'[39] Hence
it is that Nature, or God acting through Nature, 'has so
fashioned man's personality as to protect his individual autonomy, thus making possible fully personal relationships both
between man and man and between man and God'.[40] This
is instanced, for example, in the fact that 'Mind can only

communicate with mind through a reciprocal use of symbols'.[41] Nevertheless, human beings have 'an ultimate freedom to establish or avoid communication'.[42] Thoughts cannot be thrust into our minds and our intellects cannot be directly manipulated, as is the case with patients under hypnosis. Hence we are distinct and autonomous persons. It follows that communication between humans involves 'a willingness to be communicated with'.[43] It is not otherwise when the communication at issue is between man and the Divine Person. In this area, formal cognitive freedom 'becomes a material and important freedom in relation to the divine Person'.[44] There are two reasons for this. The first is the obvious one that since God is not a spatio-temporal object within the world his presence and activity could not be so obvious to us as similar objects. The second is that if we are to go on existing as distinct, autonomous and dignified persons, the nature of the Deity as an infinite Being requires that he communicate himself to us indirectly, obliquely, in a veiled fashion.[45] For God is infinite; his demand is unconditional and absolute; entering into relationship with God means a complete dismantling and reorienting of man's life. Such a radical reordering of man's outlook is such that it 'must be undergone willingly if it is not to crush and even destroy the personality'.[46] If God were to reveal himself to us coercively, he would 'annihilate us as free and responsible persons'.[47] It follows, therefore, that 'if man is to be personal, God must be *deus absconditus*'.[48] Hence man has 'the freedom either to encourage or to thwart the propensity' to interpret his environment in religious terms.[49] The reason for God's indirect revelation to us is that 'only thus can the conditions exist for a *personal* relationship between God and man'.[50]

IV.17   How is what we have been describing to be related to our concept of 'seeing as'? Hick does not think that this concept by itself is adequate for elucidating the epistemology of religion. His thesis is that 'seeing as' must therefore be expanded into the concept of 'experiencing as', 'not only visually but through all the modes of perception functioning together'.[51] The perception involved in religion differs from the reapperception involved in a Wittgensteinian puzzle picture, '. . . because the totality which it discloses constitutes a situation within which the interpreter is himself inextricably involved as a constituent, a situation which makes continual practical demands upon him'.[52] In the religious situation the entire personality is involved, including, of course, the will. Thus when the believer speaks of 'God' he is not referring to a hypothetical being whose existence is *inferred* from a religious vision of reality, but is speaking of 'the unique transcendent personal Creator of the Universe' who acts 'towards him through the circumstances of his life'.[53] This latter point of Hick's is important, because it has a bearing upon the *kind* of theistic conclusion that we think that a natural theology has – a logical construction, a Wisdomian 'greater apprehension', an ontological myth, or whatever.[54] This is a point which we shall have to reconsider at a later point (VI.39f.).

IV.18 A brief word must now be said about the positive value and function of awkward or inappropriate facts within a theistic vision of the world, a subject already opened up in connection with the views of Flew and Mitchell (cf. III.23–24 and IV.4). This question can only be discussed, in Hick's view, in the light of the purpose for which it is held that the world exists. Now Hebrew-Christian theism holds that this is to encourage 'a process through which moral personality is gradually being created by free response to environmental challenges and opportunities'.[55] Within the process human beings are called upon to develop certain inter-personal qualities (unselfishness, love, and courage) 'which are evoked by difficulties and obstacles and by situations which may demand the sacrifice of the self and its interests for the sake of others'.[56] Now free and responsible persons, able to act in freedom from outside coercion, are able to interact and to inflict sorrow and pain, happiness and unhappiness, on each other: perhaps therefore, Hick argues, our present world 'is capable of producing a far higher value in the sphere of personality than a ready-made hedonistic paradise'.[57] Of course, this cannot be proved by observation, but it remains

true that the world can be *experienced as* and *seen as* 'a vale of
soul-making' or *as* 'a fortuitous concourse of atoms'.[58] Once
more we see that the objections of Flew to theism based on facts
of evil and suffering are far from unanswerable, and that the
problem of defining a positive value and function for awkward
and inappropriate facts within a theistic vision of the world is
not insoluble.

IV.19 It is within the context of this theory of interpretation
and 'experiencing as' (IV.10–17) that Hick's parable must be
interpreted. When this is done, it is clear that there are differences, already noted, between the views of Hick and, for instance,
those of Wisdom. Similarly, when we compare the parable of
Mitchell with that of Wisdom, clear differences emerge. Nevertheless, despite these differences, hopefully enough has been said
about them all to demonstrate that there are important simi-
larities between all three, that all of them share a certain family
resemblance. When we examine these parables, together with
their various contexts, we see emerging, germinally at least, a
rough idea of how a post-analytic natural theology might be
formulated. To put this slightly differently: in each of the
parables what we have is a bare, formal, suggestive but rather
abstract and symbolic *model* for the formulation of such a natural
theology. What each parable actually speaks about in the way of
evidences for theism *symbolizes* rather than describes or analyses in
detail what the metaphysical theologian draws attention to
when he outlines his metaphysical scheme. Such symbols
include the order, purpose and beauty of Wisdom's garden, the
encouraging and trust-eliciting behaviour of Mitchell's partisan,
the refreshment, delight, encouragement and hope enjoyed by
Hick's traveller. The major and formidable task which now
faces us is to translate these parabolic symbols into the kind of
non-parabolic and non-symbolic detailed evidences which have
their proper location within a concrete natural theology, integrating them by means of some of the insights supplied by the
parables' contexts (together with insights obtained from elsewhere), in order that these evidences may be seen as severally

co-operating to show that theism is not merely a possible, but also an illuminating and compelling theory which integrates all of our experience into a rational unity. This is a task which will be tackled in the next chapter.

IV.20 Before we move on to do so there is one problem about which something must be said. We are going to be talking soon of seeing (and experiencing) the world *as* a special kind of place rather than *as* some other kind. The parables each point to an *ambiguity* which runs through the world, in that it can be regarded *as* one thing or *as* another, each parable delineating *two* competing *aspects* of what is there, the central dispute being about which of the *two* viewpoints is the most appropriate and tenable. The problem here is that many may feel that to put things in this way is to become guilty of unwarranted *over-simplification*. Why, it may be asked, stop at *two* viewpoints, *two* aspects on the world? Some who put such questions are of the conviction that the approach to the epistemology of religion we have been describing is unsatisfactory, and that one way to underline this is to show how the difficulties would be multiplied if we were indeed in the intolerable position of comparing and discriminating between not *two* but a *plurality* of viable perspectives on things. Professor H. D. Lewis, for example, who is critical of our aspectual approach to natural theology, does just this. Having discussed metaphysical theology in terms of perspectives or slants on the world, Lewis comments:

> But there are various perspectives we may have of the world, we may think of it in a Buddhist way or in a Christian way or in a Marxist way. There is nothing factually at issue here, the facts are the same for all, and likewise when some take up the Hinayana view of Buddhism and others the Mahayana, when some hold by orthodox Islam, and some become Sufi Mystics, when some become Catholic Christians and some Protestants, when some subscribe to Barthian theology and others to Modernism, there is no question of fact involved, nothing to which the distinction of true or false properly applies, but only the different slants we have on the same reality.[59]

The same kind of criticism comes from a different source. While commenting upon Wisdom's approach to philosophical theology in terms of tracing patterns in the world, Dr John Macquarrie remarks:

> The tracing of rival patterns in the world would be rather like working out rival interpretations of a play of Shakespeare. Could one ever say that this interpretation is true and another false, or does the question of truth and falsity arise in such a case? Is it perhaps the mark of a great work of art that it can yield *many patterns* to its interpreters? (Italics mine.)[60]

IV.21 *Prima facie*, this might appear as a fatal criticism, yet, on examination, it soon appears that it is based on a misunderstanding. For all that this aspectual approach to metaphysical theology insists upon is that the process of seeing as (and experiencing as) and the parabolic discussions which it generates illumine the issues involved in the classic dispute of *a supernaturalistic versus a naturalistic interpretation of the world*. None of its defenders, so far as I am aware, has ever suggested that it is applicable to the divergence of Islam into different schools of thought or to the division of Buddhism into its Southern and Northern components. But what its defenders do suggest is that it illumines helpfully the issues involved in the classic dispute as to whether we can reasonably consider the world *as* limited to the empirical, to the observable, or *as* the empirical complemented or interpenetrated by the metempirical, the unobservable, the spiritual. There is in John Hick's *Faith and Knowledge* a notable passage which illustrates this point admirably. In the context of enquiring about what he calls 'an innate religious bias of human nature' (i.e. an innate tendency in man to interpret his environment religiously), Hick enquires about what is *essentially religious*. What, he asks, is the common factor which links together taboo-beliefs and ethical theism, the Brahmanic-Hindu view of the Absolute as a non-personal Unity and the Judaic-Christian and Islamic view of the Absolute as moral personality, polytheism and monotheism, and so on? In Hick's view, the common factor is a belief.

> This is the belief (implicit or explicit) that man's environment is other and greater than it seems, that interpenetrating the natural, but extending behind or beyond or above it, is the Supernatural, as a larger environment to which men must relate themselves through the activities prescribed by their cult. The Supernatural, whether conceived as one or as many, as

good or evil or part good and part evil, as lovable or fearful, to be sought or shunned, figures in some fashion in everything that can be termed religion. And our innate tendency to interpret our world religiously is a tendency to experience it 'in depth', as a supernatural as well as a natural environment.[61]

In other words, the dispute at issue is whether a religious or a non-religious interpretation of the world is the most satisfying, the most rational and the most illuminating. This is a dispute whose roots in the West reach back into pre-Socratic Greek philosophy. It is this particular dispute alone, in the context of metaphysical theology, which, it is claimed, is clarified by the application of notions such as 'seeing as' and 'experiencing as', and no other. Nevertheless, Professor Lewis has put his finger on one problematic point which we have noted before and to which we shall have to return again: the defender of this approach to natural theology is strictly required to demonstrate *in what sense* his supernaturalistic interpretation of the world differs *factually* from the naturalistic one of his opponent.[61]

NOTES

1. See pp. 103–5; with the following section IV.1–IV.7 cf. F. Ferré, *Basic Modern Philosophy of Religion*, New York, 1967, pp. 335–49.

2. *New Essays*, p. 129.

3. The text is to be found in John Hick, *Faith and Knowledge*, Second Edition, London, 1967, pp. 177–8; *Philosophy of Religion*, Englewood Cliffs, N.J., 1963, pp. 101–2; Bowden and Richmond, *A Reader on Contemporary Theology*, pp. 149–50. For Hick's contribution to the philosophy of religion see also *Faith and the Philosophers*, London, 1964, ed. J. Hick, 'Sceptics and Believers', pp. 235–50; 'Religious Faith as Experiencing-As', in *Talk of God*, ed. G. N. A. Vesey, Royal Institute of Philosophy Lectures, Volume Two, 1967–8, London and New York, 1969.

4. '. . . We can also *see* the illustration now as one thing, now as another, and *see* it as we *interpret* it', *Philosophical Investigations*, xi, p. 193ᵉ.

5. See *Faith and Knowledge*, pp. 98–9.

6. *Op. cit.*, p. 101.

7. *Ibid.*

8. *Ibid.*, pp. 104–5.

9. *Ibid.*, p. 105.

10. *Ibid.*, p. 99.

11. *Ibid.*, p. 106.

12. *Ibid.*

13. *Ibid.*, p. 107.

14. *Ibid.*, p. 108.
15. *Ibid.*, p. 109.
16. *Ibid.*, p. 111.
17. *Ibid.*
18. 'Religious Faith as Experiencing-As', in Vesey, *op. cit.*, p. 29.
19. *Ibid.*
20. *Ibid.*, p. 30.
21. *Ibid.*
22. *Faith and Knowledge*, p. 112.
23. Vesey, p. 30.
24. *Ibid.*, pp. 30–1.
25. *Faith and Knowledge*, p. 117.
26. *Ibid.*
27. *Ibid.*, pp. 116–17.
28. Vesey, pp. 31–3; *Phil. of Rel.*, pp. 72–7; *Faith and Knowledge*, pp. 142–3.
29. *Phil. of Rel.*, p. 72.
30. *Faith and Knowledge*, p. 121.
31. *Ibid.*, p. 122.
32. *Ibid.*, p. 123.
33. *Ibid.*, p. 124.
34. *Ibid.*
35. *Ibid.*, p. 125.
36. *Ibid.*, p. 126.
37. *Ibid.*, p. 127.
38. *Ibid.*, p. 128.
39. *Ibid.*, p. 129.
40. *Ibid.*
41. *Ibid.*, p. 130.
43. *Ibid.*, p. 132.
44. *Ibid.*, p. 133.
45. *Ibid.*
46. *Ibid.*, p. 134; a similar insight plays a crucial part in the argument of Kierkegaard's *Philosophical Fragments*. Speaking of the love and of the qualitative differences between man and God, Kierkegaard says, '. . . this love is through and through unhappy, for how great is the difference between them. It may seem as a small matter for God to make himself understood, but this is not so easy of accomplishment if he is to refrain from annihilating the unlikeness that exists between them,' *Philosophical Fragments*, Princeton, 1936, p. 19.
47. *Ibid.*
48. *Ibid.*, p. 135.
49. *Ibid.*, p. 136.
50. *Ibid.*, p. 140.
51. *Ibid.*, p. 142; cf. the paper 'Religious Faith as Experiencing-As', where this expansion is treated in detail.
52. *Ibid.*, p. 143; a clear case of this is again the situation of Mitchell's partisan. See IV.3 above.
53. *Ibid.*, p. 146.

54. *Ibid.*, p. 145.

55. *Ibid.*, 158.

56. *Ibid.*

57. *Ibid.*

58.; *Ibid.* cf. Hick's extensive treatment of this in *Evil and the God of Love*, and *Phil. of Rel.*, pp. 4of.

59. *Phil. of Rel.*, pp. 100–1.

60. *Twentieth-Century Religious Thought*, p. 316.

61. *Faith and Knowledge*, p. 137.

62. Cf. A. J. Ayer, *Language, Truth and Logic*, p. 115: '. . . if the sentence "God exists" entails no more than that certain types of phenomena occur in certain sequences, then to assert the existence of a god will be simply equivalent to asserting that there is the requisite regularity in nature; and no religious man would admit that this was all that he intended to assert in asserting the existence of a god. He would say that in talking about God, he was talking about a transcendent being who might be known through certain empirical manifestations, but certainly could not be defined in terms of those manifestations.'

V

THE THEISTIC EVIDENCES

V.1 In a pregnant paper Ian Ramsey spells out in detail much of what we have hinted at above about the nature of metaphysical inquiry in general and metaphysical theology in particular.[1] In Ramsey's view, metaphysics is rooted in man's desire 'to know . . . just where he is journeying'; more particularly, 'it arises whenever man seeks to map the Universe and to plot his position upon it'.[2] One factor common to metaphysicians is their 'desire to have an outline map of the Universe, some overall scheme capable of placing whatever transitoriness brought with it'.[3] Following up a hint dropped by Whitehead, Ramsey can define the broad purpose of metaphysics: 'to elaborate some explicit interpretative scheme, critically suited as far as may be to the whole of experience'.[4] The connection between this and what we have been saying throughout earlier chapters should be so obvious as not to require comment.[5]

V.2 If we accept then that the metaphysical theologian is trying to draw an 'outline map of the Universe', to construct an 'overall interpretative scheme' in order that human experience may be structured in terms of this scheme, this question arises: which areas, regions, tracts of country, does he find significant and try to draw attention to when he indulges in this singular type of cartography? In terms used above, to which areas of human experience do the parabolic symbols refer when the metaphysical theologian translates them into the concrete, detailed evidences to which theism appeals? Our special task in this chapter is to indicate just what these areas are and just why the theist invests them with significance. In other words, we must describe those pervasive elements in human experience which generate thoughts of the ultimate, the absolute, the divine; in short, those elements which together and cumulatively generate religious beliefs. Before we tackle this task, several comments are required. The first is that in selecting and describing various areas no claim is being made that all theists would necessarily agree that this particular grouping of areas is the only or indeed the most appropriate one. Nevertheless, an attempt will be made to select a group which the majority of theists might agree is religiously significant. The second is that the subject-matter of this chapter will involve us in a reconsideration of the insights of some of the Continental thinkers whose views were briefly mentioned in our first chapter above. We argued there that although the limitations, some of them self-imposed, of much Continental (mainly German) theology have been such as to prevent it from taking the question of natural theology seriously, nevertheless such theology has been heavily pregnant with great religious insight. Hopefully, we shall soon perceive how such insights may be significantly related to the needs of the metaphysical theologian. To the areas of experience which are held to be theistically evidential we now turn in some detail.

V.3 The first area may be conveniently called, for want of a better name, the area or dimension of *religious experience*. Before this is discussed, a definition of *experience* might be helpful: Experience is 'a form of knowledge which arises from the direct reception of an impression from a reality (internal or external) which lies outside our free control. It is contrasted with that type, or aspect of knowledge in which man is an active agent, subjecting the object to his own viewpoints and methods and to critical investigation. An eminent degree of certainty ('evidence') attaches to experience since that which is experienced irresistibly attests to its own presence.'[6] We must note the insistence here that experience is a form of *knowledge*: what is experienced in this area is not quite so vague and undifferentiated that it escapes conceptualization and description altogether. The claim is made that such experience brings about an increase in our awareness of how things are; in other words, that religious experience is *cognitive*. Great importance attaches to Rahner's words '. . . which lies outside our free control'. That is, in religious experience proper, the experiential subject is convinced that what is apprehended is uninvited, unsought, un-self-induced; that it *invades* and *impinges upon* his consciousness 'from without', that it 'presses in upon him', evoking a response, that somehow it is inescapable and unavoidable. By the use of the words 'irresistibly attest its own presence' Rahner does not, I think, wish to commit himself to the heavily criticized concept of 'self-authentication' as that concept is sometimes dubiously used: rather, by using these words (and by the significant use of '*direct* reception') he is trying quite rightly to emphasize that the religious subject does not typically make an *inference from* the existence of a certain collection of inner psychic data (e.g., awe, fear, humility, shame, etc.) *to* the existence of an awe-inspiring, holy being understood as the causal explanation of such data. Rather, he claims to experience a reality directly, or, in Schleiermacher's terms, immediately, a reality known *in* and *through* the affective elements which are an inseparable ingredient of the experience.

V.4 The *locus classicus* of Western experiential religious thought is the notable German tradition from Friedrich Schleiermacher to Rudolf Otto. Even a superficial examination of the main elements of this tradition convinces us that experiential theologians have had as their aim the elucidation of the *knowledge* which is mediated in and through religious experience. But first is their attempt to *describe*, objectively and scientifically (phenomenologically), the essentials of religious experience. If we glance at Schleiermacher, for example, we find first of all a richness of *description*.[7] Schleiermacher speaks much and typically of the immediate consciousness of the eternal, of certain affections and insights evoked and generated from without, of man's being moved by the Whole which stands over against him, of the universal life contacting an individual life, of the world pressing in upon man and generating in him 'pious feeling', of the generation in man of the intersubjective, theistically significant 'feeling of absolute dependence'. Then, second, there is the attempt to elucidate conceptually what is involved in such experience. Hence Schleiermacher speaks typically of religious subjects becoming the objects of their own inquiries; of how they attempt to describe, to analyse, to schematize and conceptualize the *given* in such experience, the final product of which is to be found not only in his *Reden* but also in his monumental *Glaubenslehre*. If we consider also the work of Rudolf Otto,[8] we find these two elements, although in Otto the latter is much more highly developed than in Schleiermacher. First, there is the wealth of phenomenological description, in which is set forth the facts of the human experience of the *mysterium tremendum et fascinosum*, and, second, there is the attempt (indebted partly to Kant's philosophy of mind) to elucidate conceptually, under the key-concept of 'the Holy', what is *given* in this experience, due weight being given to both rational and suprarational elements.

V.5 It is outside the scope of this little work to sketch even in barest outline a theology of religious experience. But it may not be inappropriate to make several comments about the use of experiential evidence in theology. The experiential theologian would, I think, have to say something about the problem of the uneven frequency of occurrence of religious experiences when these are considered historically and geographically. He would concede that the religious aspect of human experience becomes most apparent when human beings are encouraged to pay attention to 'those special times or junctures in life that are set apart from the ordinary course of events and "celebrated" as having some peculiar meaning and seriousness about them'.[9] And clearly there may be times and cultures, including our own, in which such encouragement is rarely given. He could concede further, I think, that a knowledge of the great religions persuades us that religious awareness is not given to all individuals in equal degree, any more than aesthetic insight is given equally

to all. The existence of holy men, seers, gurus, and prophets in
the religions, and the use made of them by those of lesser religious endowment, show that religious awareness is not equally
bestowed on all.[10] And certainly he would argue that certain
civilizations and cultures are more sympathetic towards the
occurrence of religious experiences than others, and (perhaps)
that a civilization like our own North Atlantic technological one
is singularly unsympathetic to any such thing.[11]

V.6   But our pressing concern here is with the *empirical* and to
this we return. When the metaphysical theologian is confronted
by the sceptical empiricist what can he claim as empirical in this
area of religious experience? Briefly, he can point to countless
millions (of both past and present) claiming firmly that their
consciousness has been impinged upon and their awareness
enlarged by the uninduced pressure of something ultimate and
transcendent. This may be brought home to us by reading
through a book such as Ninian Smart's *The Religious Experience
of Mankind.*[12] It is perfectly true that the existence of such an
empirical fact alone does not prove the truth of religion or that
the interpretations put by religious subjects upon their experiences are correct. But it does something else. It points us to a
vast tract of experience of which we have to make sense, which
we have to integrate into other areas of our experience. We can
see it *as* a region of experience capable of being explained
naturalistically or *as* an aspect of the world *contingent* upon the
existence of the transcendent.[13] Let us consider, as a concrete
example, the case of one known to us who impresses us highly by
the increasing authenticity of his humanity, his intellectual
power, his moral virtue, his compassion, his selflessness, his
effect upon the community, in short, by his *saintliness*; he firmly
and explicitly claims that the development of his personal being
is rooted in his dependence upon an empirically imperceptible,
transcendent being of whom he is from time to time incorrigibly
aware, and that his religious faith makes sense of more and
more of the events of his life. His sanity is beyond all question;
indeed, his over-all personality is integrated in a fashion which

is extremely rare, an integration which he claims is rooted in the religious dimension of his experience. The question is: how are we to explain, accout for, such people and the way they are? In view of his undoubted sanity, it is hard to account for him on the grounds that he is deluded. It is hard to argue with some 'interpretation' which, it is alleged, he has put upon certain psychic data within his consciousness; for, he insists, his talk of God is not reached by inference from any data of this kind. Rather, it is descriptive of his certainty that in and through his everyday life he is being dealt with by a gracious but empirically imperceptible being. The assertion that he is just plain wrong in this over-arching conviction is discordant with everything else that we know of him. Unless for other reasons we are determined to rule religious experience out of court *a priori*, the existence of this man and the way he is constitutes a mystery for us. This mystery may be brought out by saying that his being is *contingent*, but contingent upon what? Or it might better be brought out by saying that the entire life of such a man is not *self-contained* in the sense of being *self-explanatory*. In some sense or other, we feel *compelled* (conceivably, against our will) to seek for the explanation of how this man is 'outside' of, beyond what can be spatio-temporally observed. If now we multiply the existence of this one man manyfold, we ought to be able to sense the mystery which attaches to that area or dimension of experience which we have dubbed *religious*, the first area which the metaphysical cartographer ought not to overlook.[14]

V.7 The second area may aptly be called that of *moral experience*.[15] Consideration of this area involves us in an appraisal of various forms of the so-called moral argument for the existence of God. A neater summary of the substance of moral arguments for theism can hardly be found than in the words of the late G. F. Woods:

> In the Christian tradition, the experience of communion with the ultimate has taken many forms and included many differences of emphasis but there has been a sustained tendency to find in moral experience some kind of contact with what is ultimate. In spite of moral failure and theoretical

doubts, there has been a steady tradition that men can in their finest moments of moral insight know that they are in touch with a realm of being which is sovereign over all the calculations of expediency. It is open to those who believe in these experiences to interpret them in analogical terms as communications from the ultimate being. The character of the ultimate being, the nature of its initiative, the manner in which the communication is given can all be interpreted in analogical terms derived from our own experience as personal beings.[16]

A very short summary indeed can be found in Hick's *Faith and Knowledge*:

> It is argued that the sense of obligation implies a transcendent personal will as its source and ground. The view thus baldly stated in a sentence has been set forth in impressive detail by leading religious philosophers.[17]

Generally speaking, those who regard favourably moral arguments for theism draw our attention sharply to certain momentous occasions in life when, in a situation of sharp moral conflict, we experience our consciousness being firmly impinged upon by a pressure not itself an integral part of our personality, and interpreted by us as grounded in a transcendent willing being, who stands over against us in holy, uncompromising demand.

V.8 Again, generally speaking, defenders and expounders of moral arguments are countered by those who insist that if a general, overall explanation of moral experience is to be sought, it is more reasonable and much less perplexing to seek for a naturalistic rather than a supernaturalistic one. As Hick points out, '. . . taken by themselves the facts of our ethical experience are capable of either a naturalistic or a theistic explanation. . .'[18] And Ian Crombie comments upon the matter in this way: 'Nobody who takes seriously the so-called moral argument need suppose that the *prima facie* authority of conscience cannot be naturalistically explained. He can quite well acknowledge that the imperativeness which so impresses him could be a mere reflection of his jealousy of his father, or a vestigial survival of tribal taboo.'[19] We are back once again in a situation whose structure should now by be tolerably familiar to us: that of a *naturalistic* versus a *supernaturalistic* explanation. How, in this instance, are we to make up our minds between the two? One method is to consider that if supernaturalistic explanations are intolerably perplexing, naturalistic explanations may not be less so, but more so. Elsewhere I have argued that naturalistic explanations (based upon psychological and sociological insights) provide neither an *exhaustive* or *satisfying* account of all that is involved in moral experience.[20] I cited, for example, Tillich's point 'that psychological and social pressures may provide the occasion for the making of moral judgments, but do not at all produce the unconditional dimension of the moral imperative'. Other anti-naturalistic arguments were used, including this one: 'Our moral reflection, in which we sift and criticize the concrete commands of conscience, discriminating between them and conditioned prejudices, is possible only because we are able to look at them in the light of the unconditional, the ultimate, the underived, the given.' Much was made of the fact that human beings do in fact enter into discussion in order to clear up important ethical disagreements: '. . . in fact persons do enter into ethical discussions with a view to subsequent agreement, being utterly if unconsciously convinced that moral awareness possesses an inalienable, unconditional, ultimate and underived dimension, which is the presupposed norm of such discussions, and without which they would be inconceivable.' There are other pertinent points that might be made. For example, it ought to be remembered that in everyday life much of our so-called 'moral' experience is hardly worthy of the name, being little more than unthinking, unreflective and expedient conformity to social norms. This can seriously mislead. It can conceal from us the crucial significance of qualitatively quite different situations where the moral issues are stark, frightening and heart-rending, situations which are meat and drink to the moralist and dramatist, and which ought to be so to the metaphysician. Nor ought it to be forgotten that individuals differ in the *type* of moral experience they have. Crombie has pointed out that 'there are those to whom conscience appears in the form of unconditional demand; to whom the obligation to one's neighbour seems to be something imposed on him and on me by a third party who is set over us both'.[21]

For reasons such as these we ought to be unhappy with the notion that the decision between a naturalistic and supernaturalistic explanation of the full range of moral experience is a purely arbitrary matter. It is one that can be rationally discussed and for which rational considerations may be brought forward.

V.9   Nevertheless, it must be admitted that full and final agreement on these issues is impossible to attain. But this is not important: in Crombie's words, 'All that is necessary is that he (i.e. the religious believer) should be honestly convinced that, in interpreting them, as he does, theistically, he is in some sense facing them more honestly, bringing out more of what they contain or involve than could be done by interpreting them in any other way.'[22] Even though the theist cannot here utterly refute his opponent by logical argument, he considers his theistic interpretation to be preferable on the grounds that his opponent's 'is judged to be unconvincing in the light of familiarity with the facts'.[23] What, then, can our metaphysical cartographer say, in the light of our discussion, about the area of moral experience? He can say with certainty that the area is one of mystery. He can say that in genuine (as compared with inauthentic) moral experience man has an experience of *contingency*. That is, he might say that this area also is not self-contained in the sense of being self-explanatory. Once more, he can say that he feels *compelled* to seek for an adequate explanation for moral experience 'outside' of, 'beyond', what can be empirically observed. He can argue that in drawing his outline map of our experience of the world, he must draw attention sharply to this region of moral experience as one which generates thoughts of and belief in the ultimate, the transcendent, the divine.

V.10   A third area may conveniently be called that of *human* existence.[24] The term 'existence' is here used in the technical sense which it enjoys in Continental philosophy of existence (*Existenzphilosophie*), whose father is the nineteenth-century Danish religious thinker Søren Kierkegaard. A significant characteristic of many Continental existentialist philosophers has been their allegiance to the Western religious tradition.

Kierkegaard was a Lutheran as Marcel is a Catholic; Heidegger's doctrine of man is indebted to St Augustine, Duns Scotus, Luther and Kierkegaard; the work of Karl Jaspers exhibits his admiration of the Western biblical tradition; Martin Buber was a Hasidic Jew. It is therefore not surprising that Christian theologians such as Bultmann and Tillich have looked upon the philosophy of existence as an apt vehicle for elucidating and communicating Christianity. The reason why our metaphysical cartographer dare not overlook the area of human existence is that the existentialists have given a phenomenological description of man as an inalienably *religious being*. To some of the most significant characteristics of such a description we now turn.

V.11 Broadly speaking, existentialist philosophers would all concur that so far as human (as contrasted with non-human) being is concerned, *existence precedes essence*. That is, man differs sharply from the non-human realm in that his essentiality is not given to him as an already realized possibility or as a possibility whose realization is inevitable. Rather, man's essentiality lies before him in his future as something which he has yet, by life-long effort and repeated decision, to aim at, grasp, lay hold of, realize. It follows that human essentiality cannot be adequately grasped or communicated by the natural or human sciences. Another characteristic is the emphasis placed on *fallenness* as a universal attribute of human nature. Hence the existentialist doctrine that human existents are in greater or lesser degree 'fallen away from' or estranged from their authentic or genuine mode of existence. In the Heideggerian version of fallenness, man flees from the responsibility to realize his true, genuine self by identifying himself with the average or typical member of contemporary civilization, or by understanding his life exhaustively in terms of the categories supplied by the natural and human sciences. The Jewish personalistic existentialist Buber understands fallenness as meaning man's being sunk in the impersonal, technical world of *It*, cutting himself off from the development of his personal being made possible only in *I-Thou* relationships. Different versions of the doctrine of fallenness are to be found in Marcel and Jaspers.²⁵ Such thinkers go on to speak, in their various ways, of what might be called *transition*: in Heidegger's case, from inauthentic to authentic existence; in Jaspers's, conversion to a 'philosophical faith' in which man achieves union with his genuine self and with God. Existentialist literature abounds in what have been called phenomenological analyses of 'basic affective states', of which the most significant is probably 'dread' (*Angst*). The contention is that such states are cognitive: they bring sharply to our attention certain aspects of being which are easily overlooked. For example, *dread* is considered as evoked by the totality of the human situation, bringing to light man's abhorrence of his present, empirical self and his drive towards his future, genuine self, being ever in tension between, on the one hand, finitude, and, on the other, freedom. Existentialist writers have been prominent amongst those who have been most critical of certain tendencies in our modern civilization and culture, especially in so far as these have dehumanized man and concealed from him the true nature of the human situation and predicament. Doubtless, this is a very crude and inadequate description of what is involved in the existentialist picture of human nature; yet it may be accurate enough to enable us to make several pertinent points.

V.12 The portrait of human nature as painted by modern existentialists leads us to make three connected points of significance for our study. First, that the portrait is essentially a *religious* one is demonstrated by the fact that a Christian theologian like Bultmann has utilized Heidegger's two contrasted modes of human existence (inauthentic and authentic) in order to reinterpret the Pauline corpus of the New Testament.²⁶ Second, the existentialist stress on *transition* (or *conversion*) from inauthentic or fallen to genuine or authentic existence, together with connected teachings on dread, guilt, death, conscience and so on, is thoroughly *religious* in the sense that it supplies a conceptual anthropological framework within which certain theological notions (e.g. God, grace, conversion, new life, etc.) are given a clear, cogent and relevant meaning. Third, there is a point with which existentialist theologians like Bultmann (due to anti-metaphysical bias) would not agree: it is that prolonged contemplation of the structure of human nature as disclosed by existentialist analysis may lead us to regard it as *contingent*; that is, to perceive it as pointing towards, derivative from and dependent upon some transcendent, creative, personal ground possessing those characteristics (e.g. holiness, graciousness, etc.) which traditional theism has always predicated of God.[27]

V.13 But what is the relevance of this for our metaphysical cartographer? Once more, it can be said that this third area is one of mystery. Within the context of human existence there is yet again an overwhelming experience of the contingency of the world. This area also is not self-contained in the sense of being self-explanatory. It can quite plausibly be argued that a complete, adequate and full explanation of the structure and meaning of human existence can only be achieved, however reluctantly, by moving outside or beyond the empirically observable. Hence our cartographer, drawing his outline map of our experience of the world, must include and draw attention to this area as one in which awareness of and insight into the ultimate and the transcendent are generated, one which must ultimately be significantly related to the adjoining areas of which the map as a whole is comprised.

V.14 A fourth area may be aptly called that of *history*. It is a truism that Western theistic religion is closely tied up with certain crucial historical events. It is equally truistic that recent Western theology has taken an unprecedented interest in the relationship between religious thought and history, religious thought and historiography, religious thought and the philosophy of history. Indeed, the occurrence of this interest may be said to have constituted a theological revolution of the first magnitude. But here we can only be concerned with it as it is of significance for our study.

V.15 Taking history in the rather crude and unsophisticated sense of 'a systematic study of the past', the relevance of history for the metaphysical theologian can at once be perceived. For when the theologian investigates the *past* religious history of mankind he encounters interpretative evidence in the past for his *present* interpretation of experience. He finds his present interpretation of experience to be *inter-subjective* in the sense not only that there are those in the present who share his way of looking at the world, but also that this has been shared by countless numbers of previous generations. It is a truism of modern philosophy of history (to be learned most conveniently from R. G. Collingwood's *The Idea of History*) that in investigating past-historical documents the *re-living* or *re-experiencing* of certain human events is a possibility. In other words, the experience of past generations is not a dead letter for us, forever shut off from us by the passage of time. It is also pertinent at this point to remember the later Wittgenstein's doctrine that *the meaning of a word is given by the way it is used*. If so, we cannot properly determine the meanings of key-words in religious thought (e.g. God, grace, salvation, transcendence, contingency etc.) unless we investigate not only how *they are used*, but also *how they always have been used*. Their use, past and present, constitutes their meaning for us. Terms like 'God' and 'transcendence' are not like 'molecule' or 'neutron', simply because the use of the former stretches back into pre-history; within such terms there are, so to speak, encapsulated millennia of human experience, reflection and interpretation. It follows that a-historical religious thought is not religious thought at all. To investigate man's past spiritual life (or, better, the history of man's ultimate explanation of his total experience) may once more lead us to experience strongly the *contingency* and mystery of man and his world, in the sense that we discover man's inherent inability fully to make sense of (or to give an explanation of) the totality of his experience without recourse to terms and symbols (however oblique and inadequate) which refer to non-experimental unobservables.

V.16   But clearly the term 'history' as actually used in Western religious thought means more than this. 'History' is sometimes used (e.g. by Jews) to indicate particularly the history of Israel, and by others (e.g. by Christians) to indicate particularly the history of Christ and of the experience of the Christian community, complemented by the history of Israel. This history receives interpretation. The history of historiography in recent centuries demonstrates the use of two categories of historical interpretation – namely, 'nature' and 'man'. In the nineteenth century, for example, much stress was placed on history as a sort of *natural* process whose systematic study was analogous to man's study of nature (*historicism*). Much effort was expanded towards discovering and elucidating historical processes (the rise and fall of empires, cultures, etc.), historical laws, historical generalizations, towards the formulation of historical predictions, and the like. But the modern revolution in historical thought associated with the names of Dilthey, Croce, and Collingwood introduced a strong reaction against this by emphasizing strongly the causal functions of man, his freedom and creativity, in shaping historical events and movements ('all history is the history of mind'), thus introducing the notion of human contingency into a process hitherto conceived as being a closed, cause-and-effect affair largely determined by impersonal laws and drives. This revolution portrayed history as a relatively open rather than as a deterministically sealed-off area of reality. An understanding of this revolution may help us to appreciate the modern Western theologian's attitude to history. For if history is not a closed causal system and is determinable in part by the free spiritual creativity of man is it not possible to say that it is determined also by the activities of the transcendent?

V.17 Why does the theologian regard it as reasonable to put such a question? Fully to answer this would involve giving a detailed exposition of the work of those Western theologians who have worked almost wholly within the area of elucidating a theological interpretation of history, a task which falls outside the scope of this little book. But it is not necessary to do this; all that is necessary, hopefully, is to explain the impact given by reading their works. Between the lines of such works there is to

be perceived the reasoned conviction that the more the histories
of Israel, of Christ and of the church are contemplated and
studied, the more their shape and structure are considered, the
more an attempt is made to give them some comprehensive,
overall, satisfactory explanation, the more deeply convinced we
may become that this cannot be done without reference to the
transcendent, involved in, yet lying beyond or behind history
as its creative, personal, dynamic ground, possessed of those
attributes traditionally predicated of deity. It must be noted that
such a conviction can be generated without our being committed
to the view that this or that isolated historical event is inexplicable unless we posit the scientifically incomprehensible inter-
vention of the deity in the miraculous fracture of this or that law
of nature. Theologians differ, and will continue to differ, about
the precise interpretation to be put on this or that allegedly
miraculous event. The view being defended here is that the
prolonged contemplation 'in depth' of the *totality* of saving
history (as defined above) may involve us in regarding history
as 'miraculous' in the sense that in the course of quite worldly
and profane history there may yet be discerned an intercourse
between man and the hidden, transcendent God (cf. IV.14).

V.18 Here, then, is another area for inclusion in the outline
map of our metaphysical cartographer. Yet another area, that of
history, is describable as mysterious; in this area, as in the others,
there is possible an experience of the *contingency* of the world. It
can be said of history that it, too, is not self-contained in the
sense of 'self-explanatory'. In the case of history also, we see the
interpreter, after prolonged examination, contemplation and
analysis, being *forced* (conceivably, against his will) to seek for an
adequate, overall explanation partly in terms of factors 'outside
of' and 'beyond' what is spatio-temporal and observable. Hence
history is an area within which thought of and belief in the
transcendent and the ultimate are conceived, an area which
must ultimately be fitted significantly into the overall map
or chart of experience which is our metaphysician's ultimate
aim.

V.19 A fifth area may aptly be called that of *nature*, the happy hunting-ground of traditional speculative theology. It is impossible to discuss nature in a metaphysical context without saying something about the two traditional *a posteriori* proofs of the existence of God, about which the following pertinent comment may be made. It is paradoxical that, on the one hand, no arguments in the history of philosophy have been so incisively dissected and devastatingly criticized as these two, and, on the other, that hardly a modern book has been written on speculative theology which does not give some serious consideration to them as evidences for theistic belief. The two *a posteriori* arguments, in their traditional forms, were most rigorously analysed, had their validity denied, and their reputation undermined by Hume, followed by Kant, a procedure which has been repeated in logical terms by both logical positivists and logical empiricists in the twentieth century. That the question can still be raised therefore as to their evidential value seems to indicate that these arguments may possess insights and value which their traditional logical trappings conceal rather than reveal. An attempt must now be made to elucidate in what this value consists and precisely what these insights are.

V.20 It may be more convenient to begin with the so-called teleological argument, which received its most incisive criticism in Hume's *Dialogues Concerning Natural Religion*. Yet, when we have read through and well pondered Hume's *Dialogues*, a question worth asking is this: is there anything of value left at all? Has Hume (as undergraduate essay-writers are wont to say) 'obliterated' or 'completely abolished' the argument? To answer such questions it is wise to turn to Hume himself. So far as it is possible to detect Hume's own position, we seem to find it, if anywhere, in Part XII of the *Dialogues*,[28] where he seems to concur with those who maintain that '. . . the whole of natural theology . . . resolves itself into one simple . . . proposition, *that the cause or causes of order in the universe probably bear some remote analogy to human intelligence*'. When Hume reached this conclusion he regarded it as a pleasingly minimal one, in the sense that it was, from the point of view of human life, quite vacuous; he warns us that the conclusion affords 'no inference that affects human life, or can be the source of any action or forbearance'. (Hume disliked religion, as Kemp Smith has reminded us, on the grounds that on the whole its effects on human affairs, as he had observed them, were pernicious.) Yet, on the other hand, it means that our undergraduate friends are not quite right with 'obliteration' and 'complete abolition'. What appears to have gone wrong with the teleological argument is this: its defenders have taken over an important insight into reality, and have misleadingly inserted it into a logical formulation which has been deservedly thrashed by Hume and his disciples. The insight is this: that the more we contemplate the natural order in its entirety, the more we are impressed by the remarkable order, value and regularity we find there; the prolonged contemplation of this generates in us the conviction that the sheer quantity of intelligibility we find throughout the natural world (despite disorderly and dysteleological elements) requires some kind of explanation other than mere fortuitousness.[29] In other words, there is borne in upon us irresistibly an acute sense of the *contingency* of the natural order, a sense which, while it is not derived from the conclusion of a syllogism, is not to be understood merely as an arbitrary, emotive or irrational response.[30] And the 'explanation', even on Humean grounds, must some how be in terms of a transcendent, personal (because intelligent) being involved in, yet unobservable within the spatio-temporal natural order.

V.21 Our treatment of the cosmological argument is not dissimilar. The traditional logical trappings of its various formulations are clearly open to the most serious objection. From Hume to the present day, logical and epistemological criticisms of the moves inherent in the first three of St Thomas's *Five Ways* (from Motion to a Prime Mover, from Causality to a First Cause, from Contingency to a Necessary Being) have accumulated devastatingly.[31] Nevertheless, it remains arguable that underlying and perhaps concealed by the traditional dress of the argument is an important insight incapable of syllogistic formulation. This is perhaps that the more that we contemplate all that there is, concentrating attention closely upon change, flux, movement, activity, the ceaseless and throbbing dynamism inherent in things wherever we look, we arrive at that point where we perceive that all that there is is not 'self-contained', and must be explicable (if explicable it is) in terms of the activity of an ultimate and personal transcendent being, ultimate and personal in the sense that the activity of such a being is underived, creative and *sui generis*. In other words, our prolonged contemplation in depth of all that there is leads once more to the overwhelming conviction of its *contingency*.

V.22 Nature is therefore another area which our metaphysical cartographer cannot afford to overlook in his construction of an overall map of experience, in so far as here once again is an area which is inexplicable in itself, in its own terms. Once more the interpreter, the longer he looks and the more prolonged his contemplation, comes to that point where he is forced to seek for an explanation of what he experiences as mystery 'outside of' or 'beyond' what is empirically observable, an area which must yet be significantly related to juxtaposed areas of the total map which is the ultimate aim of the exercise.

V.23 The point has now perhaps been reached, due to considerations of space, where a halt must be called to this exercise of delineating significant areas or regions of human experience. It must again be stressed that the choice of such areas is somewhat arbitrary, in the sense that there are those who would protest not only against significance omissions but also against the varying degrees of emphasis placed upon one or more areas at the expense of others. One can conceive of protests directed against, for example, the omission of the *aesthetic* area from consideration. Others, again, might protest that moral arguments are, in their view, intolerably defective or unconvincing. Others might be of the opinion that Continental existentialism in most of its varieties is much too obscure and anti-rational to deserve serious consideration. Nor would it be totally unreasonable for the disciple of, say, Martin Buber to complain of the intolerable omission of what Buber called the 'interhuman' (*zwischenmenschliche*) area of reality, that aspect through which, above all others, in their view, man comes to God. The Thomist may reasonably complain that the treatment given to nature is far too cursory and brief to do justice to the persuasive subtlety of Aquinas. I should agree, and can only refer enquirers to the books of Dr Farrer and Dr Mascall, where the notion of the *contingency* of the natural order is communicated with great power in technical detail. Most seriously of all, perhaps, the revelationist has grounds for complaint. For, will he not ask, is it not the case that awareness of the divine and the transcendent is most typically reached, not through the efforts of the interpreter trying to grasp the hem of God's garment, but through the overwhelming and acknowledged pressure of the transcendent upon man? Why, then, the omission of the area of *revelation*? Once again, I can but agree, although it would be pertinent to point out not only that the category of revelation may already have been hinted at in connection with religious and moral experience and with history, but also (wickedly) that a heavy stress on revelation in the past has not uncommonly been accompanied by a (sometimes concealed) plea that philosophical reflection is, in the presence of revelation, either incompetent, impudent or gratuitous. But the comprehensive reply to all protesters is this: the delineation of significant areas of experience undertaken above has been done only to suggest a *model* for this cartographical approach to the experienced world, and for no other reason. No claim is made that the delineation here sketched is the only or indeed the best one. No doubt alternative and more convincing groupings can be hit upon. This does not matter: so long as the delineation carried out adequately suggests a satisfactory model for structuring our experience of the world and so long as it adequately conveys something of what it means to experience, sense or glimpse the *contingency* of the world as given to experience, it will have fulfilled its purpose.

V.24 We have mentioned once more the term 'contingency', and this mention brings us to the last difficulty to be dealt with in this chapter, albeit a formidable and, some would argue, a fatal one. For 'contingency' has turned out to be something of a key-word in this chapter, and it is notoriously a very obscure word indeed. For, as I. M. Crombie has pointed out,[32] the term 'contingent' (and its opposite 'necessary') has been taken over by logicians as applicable only to *propositions*. A contingent statement is one that might be either true or false (there is no 'necessity' about it; a necessary statement is necessarily true in the sense that to deny its truth is to involve oneself in logical contradiction, since the statement is true by definition or convention). But, Crombie points out, *all* statements referring to existence are contingent, and this must apply to theistic statements also. (We could only think of a statement referring to the divine existence being necessarily true if we accepted one of the forms of the ontological argument.) Crombie suggests that the theist who speaks of 'the contingency of the world' must have borrowed the word from the logician and is using it now in a new way, a way which is intolerably unclear. For if all existential statements except theistic ones are contingent, why should an exception be made of these latter ones? In other words, why should everything we experience be contingent except God? What does it mean to speak of God as being non-contingent?

V.25 Crombie admits that it is arguable that the metaphysical use of 'contingent' may be earlier in the history of thought than its use in modern logic, and it may be helpful to enquire about the logic which underlies its former use. If we can grasp this, it may be that we shall sense something of what 'contingent' means in a religious context. Clearly the term was common in mediaeval Catholic theology and was used, for example, by St Thomas in the third of the Five Ways (V.21). Karl Rahner tells us that by 'contingency' in philosophical theology is meant '. . . the fortuitous character, . . . the non-necessity, of an existing being, for essence and existence are distinct and not necessarily united'.[33] Rahner continues, '. . . when existence is not part of the nature of a thing, so that its mere being there before us is enigmatic, that thing refers us to some outside principle which must explain why essence and existence are in fact united here ... thus plainly revealing itself to be produced and sustained by the absolute being of God, incapable of existing without him, or of being affirmed unless he be (implicitly) affirmed'. This rather abstract definition perhaps becomes clearer when we apply it to our discussion of the various areas of experience, and to those ways in which this experience throws us 'beyond' or 'outside' the empirical world for some kind of explanation, since what is disclosed to us in experience is 'mysterious' in the sense of being fragmentary and not self-explanatory. But what does Rahner mean by the 'absolute' being of God? Elsewhere, he defines the absolute as 'That which exists in and of itself altogether exempt of any dependence. In general the absolute is conceived as existing of itself, as true of itself, and as good of itself, without dependence of any kind.'[34] In the context of our present study this means that experience throws us beyond the empirical towards an explanation which is ultimate and absolute in the sense that *beyond it we cannot go*; there can be no explanation of *this* explanation. An absolute or ultimate explanation is one in terms of something which is (in Rahner's sense) exempt from dependence of any kind; that is, in terms of something or some being not itself generated or determined by anything 'more ultimate'. Hence the explanation at issue is in terms of a transcendent personal being, conceived of as ultimate or absolute, who exists of himself 'without dependence of any kind'. Receiving his existence *from himself*, he could not conceivably cease to exist through the activity (or lack of it) of any 'more ultimate' being or principle. (The Aristotelian term 'Unrestricted Act' is not altogether inept here.) Hence it can be said that this being exists *necessarily* (unrestrictedly and independently) while the finite world exists *contingently* (derivatively and dependently). We must note that the meaningfulness of this account depends on two related conditions. The first is that the conception of a transcendent personal being is shown to be really and truly *explanatory*. It must be shown that this conception does in fact satisfactorily illumine a perplexing state of affairs. The second is that the explanation can plausibly be regarded as ultimate: if the explanation at issue can be shown to be interim (in the sense that at a later date it may be superseded) or penultimate, then clearly the account must fail.[35] Hopefully, this account casts some light upon what is meant by the 'contingency' of the finite world and the 'necessity' of a self-existent personal being.[36]

V.26 Perhaps a little more can be said to get the puzzled enquirer to sense what is meant by 'contingency'. We can fall back once more on the Wittgensteinian rule that 'the meaning of a word is given by the way it is used'. The implication is that the word can only be understood in the context of actual statements and sentences in which it is used. It follows that the word 'contingency' can only be understood in so far as we ponder it in relation to the various phrases which we have used, such as 'not self-contained', 'not self-explanatory', 'mysterious', 'fragmentary', 'being thrown outside or beyond the empirically observable', 'the world as pointing towards, derivative from, and dependent upon a transcendent, personal, creative ground'. The word 'contingent' attempts to fuse and convey what these mean as components of a certain kind of experience of the world. It may be therefore that if we keep these explanations in mind we shall be able to use the word 'contingency' with a tolerable amount of clarity.[37]

NOTES

1. 'On the Possibility and Purpose of a Metaphysical Theology', in *Prospect for Metaphysics*, pp. 153–77.
2. *Op. cit.*, p. 153; cf. III.3f. above.
3. *Ibid.*, pp. 153–4.
4. *Ibid.*, p. 154.
5. With Ramsey's views on metaphysics as a kind of anthropological cartography it is illuminating to compare parallel views; cf. W. H. Walsh, *Metaphysics*, London, 1963, 'Metaphysics and Practice', pp. 195f.
6. Rahner/Vorgrimler, *Concise Theological Dictionary*, p. 162.
7. See *On Religion: Speeches to Its Cultured Despisers*, tr. by John Oman, New York, 1958, 'Second Speech – the Nature of Religion'.

8. *The Idea of the Holy*, Oxford, 1923.

9. John E. Smith, *Experience and God*, New York, 1968, pp. 57f.

10. '. . . The religious awareness of different individuals varies greatly in degree of coherence. At one extreme it is spasmodic, diverse, and wavering; at the other extreme (perhaps an ideal limit) it is present through life, colouring uniformly the whole continuum of experience', in *Faith and the Philosophers*, p. 245.

11. See H. D. Lewis, *Phil. of Rel.*, pp. 148f.

12. New York, 1969.

13. For a discussion of how 'contingent' is used in our discussion, see V.24f. below.

14. Cf. John Macquarrie, *God-Talk*, London, 1967, pp. 236–7.

15. With V.7 cf. my *Faith and Philosophy*, chapter III, 'The Moral Route to Theistic Belief'.

16. *Theological Explanation*, pp. 146–7; a fuller account of Woods's views on this subject may be found in *A Defence of Theological Ethics*, Cambridge, 1966.

17. P. 159.

18. *Ibid.*

19. *New Essays in Philosophical Theology*, p. 112.

20. *Faith and Philosophy*, pp. 117f.

21. *New Essays*, pp. 111–12.

22. *Ibid.*, p. 112.

23. *Ibid.*

24. With V.10f. cf. my article 'Existentialism' in *A Dictionary of Christian Theology*, pp. 124–6, and *Faith and Philosophy*, chapter V, 'God and Human Existence'.

25. See *A Dictionary of Christian Theology*, p. 125.

26. See Bultmann's *Theology of the New Testament*, vol. I, London, 1952: chapter IV, 'Man prior to the Revelation of Faith', and chapter V, 'Man under Faith'.

27. Bultmann and Tillich stand firmly within the Protestant-Lutheran tradition. But the existential picture of man as a *contingent* being, a being whose structure points beyond itself to some transcendent, creative and fulfilling ground, is to be found also in Continental Catholic theology. See, for example, Karl Rahner's essay, 'Nature and Grace', printed in *Nature and Grace*, London and New York, 1963, pp. 3–44. Rahner there discusses the problem of defining 'raw' human nature, i.e. human nature considered as absolutely devoid of supernatural grace. Rahner's view is that nature is essentially 'open' to grace, pointing towards grace as its goal and fulfilment. In speaking of this fulfilment, Rahner writes: '. . . In spite of the difficulty of distinguishing what is "nature" and what isn't, nature is not thereby overthrown. The beginnings of this fulfilment already exist – the experience of infinite longing, radical optimism, discontent which cannot find rest, anguish at the insufficiency of material things, protest against death, the experience of being an object of a love whose absoluteness and whose silence our mortality cannot bear, the experience of fundamental guilt with hope nevertheless remaining, etc. Because these beginnings are brought to absolute fulfilment

by the power of God's grace, this means that in them we experience *both* grace and nature,' *Nature and Grace*, p. 36. Cf. Rahner's essay, 'Concerning the Relationship Between Nature and Grace', *Theological Investigations*, volume I, London, 1961, pp. 297–317.

28. Oxford edition, ed. N. Kemp Smith, p. 281.

29. For a modern re-statement of the teleological argument, see F. R. Tennant, *Philosophical Theology*, Cambridge, 1930 and 1968, vol. II.

30. We note that the problem could be tackled in terms of Wisdomian logic examined earlier, by going over the evidence again and again, tracing patterns, drawing connections, concentrating of features which 'severally co-operate' in favour of a theistic conclusion, grouping evidences which cumulatively point towards the conclusion aimed at, etc. With this cf. this passage from Wisdom's 'The Logic of God': 'One cannot see power but it's from what we see that we know that power is present when we watch the tube-train mysteriously move towards the Marble Arch, and the more we watch, the more explicable the mystery becomes, the more, without limit, the proof becomes a demonstration. Each day a thousand incidents confirm the doctrine that energy is indestructible: and if the present proof is not a demonstration that is not because the conclusion calls for reasons of a kind we never get. It is because the doctrine is infinite in its implications so that beyond any conceivable evidence at any time there is still evidence beyond that time – evidence for or evidence against – until no wheels are turning and time stops. In the same way, as the scroll of nature unrolls the proof of an eternal God prevails – or fails – until on the day of judgment doctrine, like theory, must become a verdict and all be lost or won', *Paradox and Discovery*, pp. 12–13.

31. See Anthony Kenny, *The Five Ways: St Thomas Aquinas' Proofs of God's Existence*, London, 1969.

32. For what follows, see the discussion of 'contingency' by I. M. Crombie, *New Essays in Philosophical Theology*, pp. 114–15.

33. Rahner/Vorgrimler, *Concise Theological Dictionary*, pp. 99–100.

34. *Ibid.*, p. 11.

35. It is illuminating at this point to consult G. F. Woods, *Theological Explanation*, chapter XIII, 'Ultimate Analogical Explanation', pp. 132–51.

36. It could be argued that metaphysical theists, once they have found an adequate, comprehensive and compelling explanation of all experience in the existence of a transcendent personal ground of the world, would find it psychologically (but hardly logically) inconceivable that God should not exist. John Hick, in the context of a discussion of the ontological argument, has this to say: '. . . Was it not to the biblical writers inconceivable that God should not exist, or that he should cease to exist, or should lose his divine powers and attributes? Would it not be inconceivable to them that God might one day go out of existence, or cease to be good and become evil? And does not this attitude involve an implicit belief that God exists necessarily and possesses his divine characteristics in some necessary manner? The answer, I think, is that it was to the biblical writers psychologically inconceivable – as we say colloquially, unthinkable – that God might not exist, or that his nature might undergo change. They were so vividly aware of God that they

were unable to doubt his reality . . .', *The Many-Faced Argument*, eds. John Hick and Arthur McGill, London, 1968, p. 344. Hick continues: 'Nevertheless, the biblical tradition, in its subsequent theological development, does contain an increasingly explicit understanding of God as necessary being. In this concept it is not logical but ontological or factual necessity that is attributed to the object of man's worship' (p. 345). It is therefore possible to distinguish between logical necessity and contingency on the one hand, and their psychological, factual and ontological counterparts on the other.

37. 'The contingent-necessary distinction can . . . be interpreted in more ways than one. "A sense of contingency" may be a sense of dependence, derivativeness, or creatureliness. With these as starting-points an argument may be attempted to God as Cause or Creator and Sustainer', R. W. Hepburn, *A Dictionary of Christian Theology*, p. 73.

VI

THE THEISTIC CONCLUSION

VI.1 We return to our metaphysical cartographer. In his attempt to sketch an overall map of experience within which to read his position, he has selected and described various areas or regions of telling significance. In his attempt to describe and explain each area he has come up firmly against what we have called their 'contingency'. In each case he has been thrown bafflingly 'beyond' the empirical in his attempt to explain. In this sense, each area has turned out to be somewhat 'fragmentary' and 'mysterious'. Now there is strong reason to believe that the notion of the 'contingency' of the world, its perplexingly mysterious and tantalizingly fragmentary character, provides a starting-point for a natural theology which may be singularly relevant and attractive in the contemporary cultural situation. It is worth remembering here some words of Howard Root:

> Where do we look now for faithful, stimulating, profound accounts of what it is to be alive in the twentieth century? The inevitable answer to that question carries a judgment. We look to the poet or novelist or film producer. In creative works of art we see ourselves anew, come to understand ourselves better and come into touch with those sources of imagination which should nourish efforts in natural theology. The best text-books for contemporary natural theologians are not the second-hand theological treatises but the living works of artists who are in touch with the springs of creative imagination.[1]

Beside this we may place some recent comments on natural theology by Dr E. L. Mascall. Having given his opinion that in future Christian theism will have to display flexibility if it is to remain relevant and attractive, he continues: 'I would, however, suggest that the most hopeful starting-point will probably be found in some aspect or another of the insufficiency of the finite world.'[2] In Mascall's view, one significant theme of the present century's notable literature has been 'the insufficiency of the finite world and its incapacity to satisfy either the intellect or appetites of man'.[3] Authors (all of them atheists) cited by Mascall to support this contention include Kafka and Sartre, who have expressed in literary form 'the conviction that neither human life nor the world of which man is a part makes any sense *of itself*'.[4] Neither human life nor the world 'carries *within itself* anything that can answer the questions or satisfy the appetites that *its existence provokes*'.[5] Hence Mascall, although he admits that the contingency or absurdity of the world provide no more than a mere starting-point for theistic apologetic, goes on to contend that 'there is more hope for theism when it is recognized that a world interpreted without reference to God is absurd than when it is claimed that a world interpreted without referenee to God makes perfectly good sense'.[6] If Mascall is right, it is clear that our language which refers to the 'contingency' of the experienced world, to the absence of final explanations 'inside' the world, and the search for such 'beyond' or 'outside' the world (however puzzling and unsatisfactory they may be), cannot be quite so unintelligible as some might argue.

VI.2   But our concern in this chapter is with the theistic conclusion to be derived from those factors which we have described, and to that we return. How can our metaphysical cartographer communicate at this point with his sceptical opponent? First, it is not inconceivable that he might, by describing, delineating and analysing significant areas of experience, induce in his opponent the ability to share his point of view, to glimpse the world as he does, to occupy sympathetically, if only momentarily, the same standpoint. He might, that is, get his opponent to adopt (imaginatively, at least) the same conspectus, map, grid; to share the same or a very similar slant on the world. If so his partner in dialogue might be able to see why he holds the religious beliefs that he does, why he regards the world as a sacred place. At this level, he might even be persuaded that the overall map, framework or picture is certainly one within which, were it accepted, it is reasonable to look for and accept a special, concrete revelation of God. Yet, it must be asked, cannot a more philosophical case for belief in God be made out?

VI.3 Clearly, God is not an observable *within* the map: classical theism and orthodox empiricism are both agreed on this. This means that belief in and discourse about God are concerned not with establishing the existence of another worldly fact or with a further hitherto unnoticed factual constellation within the world of experience, but with the transcendent ground, condition and explanation of all finite existence. Hence (at a rather crude and unsophisticated level) the religious believer might argue in this way: the overall picture (or map) is such that without God it lacks coherence, meaning, and completion; the overall picture points to God as origin, ground and goal; the overall picture makes a strong claim on us to believe in God; the overall picture is transparent to God; the overall picture, upon prolonged contemplation in depth, reveals God as the ground and condition of our experience. Now admittedly these statements are rather unrefined and crude. Can we go on to clarify them in more sophisticated terms? It may be illuminating at this point to set down several quotations from a most suggestive paper by I. M. Crombie, and ponder them well, for they sum up admirably what the theist is hinting at when he talks of God.[7] While discussing the conception of the divine, in the context of an attempt to fix the reference to theistic statements, Crombie says this: 'The conception of the divine is the notion of a complement which could fill in certain deficiencies in our experience, that could not be filled in by further experience or scientific theory-making; and its positive content is simply the idea of something (we know not what) which might supply those deficiencies.'[8] Theistic expressions, Crombie contends, 'stand for the abstract conception of the possibility of the removal of certain intellectual dissatisfactions which we may feel about the universe of common experience'.[9] It would be easy to misunderstand Crombie here and imagine, quite wrongly, that he is

talking about the discredited 'filling in of gaps' in our knowledge with theological materials, but the paper as a whole makes
it clear this is not so. He insists that he is fixing the reference-
range of theological statements *for the critic*, for 'the man who
says that he cannot see what religious people are talking about',
that he is offering to perplexed sceptics a 'neutral account of
what "God" stands for, one which does not employ any notions
whose understanding presupposes a religious outlook'.[10] Within
the context of this account, Crombie's use of terms such as
'deficiencies in experience', 'intellectual dissatisfactions',[11] and
'complement' convey admirably what we have been hinting at
in our discussion of the origins of belief in and discourse about
God. He is here occupying, that is, the standpoint of the natural
theologian.

VI.4　Also, the problem may be approached from a Wisdomian standpoint with Wisdomian techniques. In this context,
our cartographer could, *vis-à-vis* his sceptical critic, run and
re-run over those areas of the map selected as significant, under-
scoring and highlighting those features of each area which, in
Wisdom's terms, 'severally co-operate in favour of' a theistic
conclusion. Hence our cartographer seeks for theistic premises
which have a cumulative effect. He would therefore run over
the areas of religious and moral experience, of human existence,
history and nature, in each case underlining distinctive and
telling features, the experience of the 'uninduced, free approach
of a reality' here and there and over there; the experience of an
'uninvited pressure' not merely in this area but in that one and
again in yet another one; the experience of 'contingency',
'mystery' and 'inexplicability' in area upon area; the experience
of 'demand' or 'holiness' not only here, but there and yet again
elsewhere. In this way evidence is accumulated upon evidence.
But he can do more. He can employ Wisdom's 'Connecting
Technique'. In so doing he *connects up* contingency in these areas
with contingency in that one, the experience of 'uninvited
pressure' here with the same kind of experience there and yet
again over there, and so on. Again, the category of the 'per-

sonal', or of 'holiness', can be used as cartographical *connectors*. Nor must our cartographer overlook the importance of the 'Disconnecting Technique'. His work must also involve breaking up or dismantling connections which he regards as inappropriate. For example, if his opponent attempts exhaustively naturalistic accounts of religious experience, of moral experience and of human existence, our cartographer is then involved in demonstrating that each of these is not merely inconclusive but also does not do justice to the experienced facts; he would be involved in invalidating theories and explanations potentially usable as *connectors* in the production of an overall map (a naturalistic one) which he feels is inappropriate to the totality of experience. In Wisdom's words, he would here be 'removing a blindness, inducing an attitude which is lacking, reducing a reaction that is inappropriate'. But he must not lose sight of his ultimate objective, which is to *connect up*, by the establishment of rhythms, patterns, and relations, the various, disintegrated, ontologically diverse areas of the overall map into a coherent whole, whose *total* significance or meaning is expressible only in utterances of a definitely theistic kind. This brings us to yet another key-word of our discussion, which is *integration*. For our cartographer has been involved in *connecting up*, linking or knitting together various experiential areas into a significant whole: in short, in *integrating* things by means of significant *integrators*. These words, *integrate*, *integrators* and *integration* have been quite widely used in recent religious thought, and we now turn to consider several of these uses in the context of natural theology.

VI.5 The terms 'integrate' and 'integration' are fairly widely used, for instance, in North American religious thought. An interesting use of the terms is to be found in a recent lecture, on the relation between religion and empiricism, by the Yale philosopher John E. Smith.[12] In this lecture Smith argues that the conception of experience to be found in latter-day English empiricism, in which experience is practically equated with sense-experiences, is incapable of doing justice to religion. His conviction is that if religion is approached in the light of the 'pragmatic empiricism' associated with the names of Peirce, James and Dewey, we find that 'there are untapped resources for interpreting religion in the broader and richer view of experience developed by the classical American philosophers'.[13] If we apply this view to religion we see 'that experience is understood as the record and result of complex interactions between the human organism as language-using animal and the environment in which that organism lives and moves'.[14] Such philosophers, Smith contends, broke with modern positivists through their insistence that experience does *not* disclose to us 'the singular, the sensible and the immediately present'; to the contrary, experience 'is inclusive of generality' and passes 'beyond atomic, sensible particulars'.[15] In order to understand how it does so we must consider two terms, namely 'context' and 'tendency'. To take the first of these, 'context' refers to the fact that experience 'reflects the many ways in which reality can be approached'; the experiencing subject is capable of seeing both himself and the world 'in many different *contexts*'. In experience, we do not only come to know *what* is there in the world, but we experience things 'many times over in different universes of meaning'.[16] Experience must therefore be understood as including 'frameworks for interpreting'. The connections between this view of experience and the view of experience as 'experiencing as' are all too obvious.

VI.6   The second term 'tendency' conveys the conviction that in experience we are not merely sensible of discrete units and things, but that we are also aware of 'their flowing into each other, of clustering together or of succeeding each other in various purposeful patterns'. Thus experience must be understood as possessing 'continuity' and 'directionality'.[17] It is mistaken, therefore, to suppose that 'experience is wholly, or even primarily a matter of theoretical knowledge'.[18] Experience is something in which we participate, something which 'we suffer and undergo, we enjoy, appreciate and live in our experience'. We are no merely detached observers of a scene; rather, 'we see ourselves as taking part in things and we regard the world as the scene of our self-realization'. The connections between this view of experience and our descriptions of 'existential involvement' above, and metaphysics as an anthropologically motivated enterprise, are so obvious as hardly to require comment.

VI.7 Smith's thesis is that if religion is approached in the light of experience so understood, much more justice is done to it than is possible with other, narrower, forms of empiricism. Experience so defined has a 'religious dimension' in so far as it raises sharply the question of an 'ultimate ground for our existence', the question of God.[19] But before exploring this issue, Smith tackles an important misunderstanding of the experiential approach to God which he wishes to defend. He will have no truck with the idea that experience leads to *mere subjectivity*. This is a misunderstanding based on the erroneous idea that the 'subjectivity' of experience implies that experience may be reduced to 'the feeling content of private consciousness'.[20] Hence the suspicion shown by dogmatic theologians for experiential theology, based on the notion that 'experience precludes, in principle, the possibility of divine transcendence'.[21] Smith regards this suspicion as baseless, for two reasons. First, it overlooks that experience may be 'disclosure of a reality transcending the experience of each individual'.[22] It does not follow that what is disclosed can be *transformed* into a set of mental representations present only within the immediate consciousness of a single observer. Second, from the fact that a reality (e.g. God) is ingredient in experience (i.e. in the experience of more than one invididual) in several different ways it does not follow that it 'can be wholly identified with or reduced to that ingredience'. In brief, '... experience does not imply the total immanence of any of its ingredients'.[23]

VI.8 For Smith, the problem of God becomes apparent only when '... we question the *from whence* of our life and the *to whence* of our striving'. In other words, when we 'raise the question and have a concern about the ultimate boundaries of our being'.[24]

(The similarity between the problem so defined and anthropological map-making is obvious.) The religious dimension of life becomes apparent only when we experientially encounter 'the question and concern for the quality of our life and our world *taken as a whole*'.[25] In the actual business of living we become aware of life diversified into 'specific and limited areas and aspects' each of which produces questions, problems, perplexities and anxieties.[26] (We are reminded here, perhaps, of the *contingency*, the mystery, which inheres in each of the areas of experience described above.) From this we come to see that 'total life is problematic'. The only solution to this problem is to find a 'self-integrating power', and the problem thus defined is the problem of God viewed from its experiential aspect.[27] The implication is that the danger which continuously threatens human life is that of self-disintegration; hence the object of the religious quest is to find an *ultimate* object of devotion capable of 'integrating and unifying the many powers and potentialities of our personal being'. An examination of human history reveals that notable attempts have been made to achieve this through theoretical and practical allegiance to some penultimate object, such as science or the State; but the examination also reveals 'the inescapability of man's problematic situation as one who stands in need of a power of self-integration'.[28] For the finite, conditioned and penultimate nature of these has thrown into prominence the ineluctable pervasiveness of the religious question, '. . . as the problem of finding the supreme object of devotion which alone has the power to overcome the forces that threaten to undo us'.[29]

VI.9 We turn to now examine the theological use of such terms as 'integration' and 'integrators' in the work of Ian T. Ramsey.[30] We have already alluded to Ramsey's view of metaphysics as a form of cartography in which man attempts to plot his cosmic position (V.1). We must now examine this view in a little more detail. In Ramsey's view, the metaphysician's ultimate aim is to draw some kind of language-map by means of which he may understand the Universe as a whole.[31] He thinks that we can best understand what this would be like if we consider three types of non-metaphysical language-maps which share certain characteristics with a metaphysical one, namely, mathematics, logic and scientific theory.[32] The point about mathematics is that it *unites* what is apparently diverse, aiming at 'wide sweeps of generalization': thus, mathematical formulae dealing with the spherical *link* talk 'about the billiard ball with talk about oranges, about the earth, about the Association (but not a Rugby) football, about tennis balls, squash balls, raindrops and suet dumplings'. Yet mathematics is only an 'ancillary scheme': there is much in the universe that falls outside its scope, that cannot be *integrated* by means of it. In the case of logic, much the same is true. For, in the last analysis, logic also is but an ancillary scheme; the formal logician's aim, according to P. F. Strawson, is to produce a highly exact language which will as adequately and comprehensively as possible map ordinary usage; yet, he realizes that his aim is unrealizable, in that although the language-map (logic) does describe and elucidate much ordinary language, yet much of this eludes this description, because of its inherently 'un-mappable' complexities. The importance of this insight is that it links up with the nature of metaphysical language, in so far as the latter also both touches and diverges from ordinary usage. Likewise also, scientific theories are complex language-maps which enable us to draw *connections* between ontologically diverse and problematic areas, to see these areas under the aspect of a larger and more comprehensible whole, thus resolving our perplexities.

VI.10 Ramsey echoes much of what we have been saying and claiming when he expounds his view that metaphysics, understood as a very large-scale language-map, brings *clarification* and *illumination* to common-sense language.[33] But we must be careful in talking of metaphysics in this way. For if it is comparable to mathematics and scientific theory in some ways, does this not mean that metaphysics is some sort of 'high-grade scientific theory'?[34] (Scientific theory, for example, is able to do a considerable amount of integration on its own by means of concepts like mass, velocity and energy.)[35] The answer to this is that an integrating-language must be such that it uses words to *integrate* two logically diverse languages which are derived from neither: in other words, the integrating linguist must aim at a 'new' language, 'new' in the sense that it 'is an alternative to, and does *not* incorporate, the former disintegrated and separate languages'.[36] This means that gains in generality and comprehensiveness seem 'to be at the expense of particularity'. In the sciences, the business of integrating diverse languages consists 'of *replacing* diversity by more generalized and less diverse schemes'. Good examples of such *integrators* (used in the past as the bases of metaphysical schemes) are *Matter* and *Evolution*. But, Ramsey contends, apparently metaphysical concepts cannot be so if they have been thrown up by purely scientific discourse; such discourse refers only to situations concerning spatio-temporal observables; hence, it follows that scientific words used as integrators are far too limited to link up not merely scientific areas but also non-scientific ones, since metaphysics inherently seeks to 'understand the whole Universe'. In Ramsey's view, metaphysical discourse must refer to 'more than observables', to 'what is more than spatio-temporal', to 'the unseen'.[37]

VI.11 But where do we seek for the origins of metaphysical words and symbols? Ramsey, as we shall see presently, points pre-eminently to the sphere of personal being for these. But they may be sought in many areas of the world – for instance, Ramsey thinks, in the sphere of ethics (V.7).[38] ' "Duty",' says Ramsey, 'may arise as a metaphysical category.' This may be seen by thinking of those situations where men have used discourse such as *Absolute* Duty, Goodness and Perfection; these are appropriate labels for situations 'in which there was no possibility of any other than a single unambiguous, unmistakable response'. Indeed, the disclosure involved in such a situation 'is one which closely resembles in its character the disclosure to which theists appeal when they speak of "God".' Ethics requires language concerning 'response', and in so far as such response is regarded as being evoked by some 'transcendent challenge', there is thrown up a key-metaphysical word like 'Duty'.[39] But Ramseyan disclosure-situations are more diverse than this. They can occur, for example, in our contemplation of *nature* (V.19f.). Such contemplation (involving, for instance, causal sequences) can make us aware of some 'other', more than spatio-temporal, more than observable (V.21). Ramsey interprets the traditional proofs of God's existence as somewhat crude attempts to elicit the disclosure of the 'unseen', of the 'unobservable', within the context of contemplating the objectively given (V.20f.).[40] The proofs thus 'approach the one concept "God" from diverse directions', or, in terms used in our earlier discussion, within diverse 'areas' of the world.

VI.12 This brings us to the use of the key-word 'God' within metaphysical theology. In the attempt to construct a single, comprehensive, all-embracing map of the world, various discrete and unconnected metaphysical words are thrown up – such as the word 'I', the word Duty', and (although Ramsey does not mention it) the word 'contingency'; there are others also, all referring to 'unobservables' which are more than spatio-temporal which refer, in brief, to the 'unseen'. The use of the word 'God' derives its justification from the fact that it 'is such an admirable integrator'.[41] The word 'God' is of such a kind that only it can *integrate* the area of personal being with the area of morals, and both of these with the area of nature, and all of them with others besides. Key-metaphysical words are structurable and organizable only in relation to the key-term 'God'. It appears to be the only word which furnishes us with a really large-scale metaphysical map covering the entire Universe, in which *all* (and not merely *some*) areas are connected up into a significant and explanatory whole.

VI.13 The connection between what Ramsey is saying here (and elsewhere) and our earlier discussions should be so apparent as not to need much further elucidation. In his attempt comprehensively to map the experienced world, our cartographer has marked out and explored various ontologically distinct regions or areas. His prolonged examination of each has brought him ineluctably to that point where he has experienced its mystery and contingency: each has appeared to him to require explanation in terms of what lies outside, beyond what is observable. He has therefore become involved in *connecting up* (Wisdom) or *integrating together* (Smith and Ramsey) these areas into a meaningful whole, in 'complementing' his experience of the world as a whole (Crombie). In doing so, he has been obliged to commit himself to the notion of an unobservable, non-spatio-temporal, personal being who, although somehow 'involved in' each of the areas, is yet 'more than' each or all of the areas; that is, who transcends them and the world which they severally constitute. In other words, his cartographical attempt to chart the experienced world as a whole has involved him in constructing a metaphysical picture, vision or scheme of a thoroughly theistic type. Yet, in having done so, he is by no means out of the wood. For what may be his most formidable difficulty yet lies before him. To this we must now turn.

VI.14 The difficulty, which is most likely to originate with a sceptical empiricist, is this. The empiricist may legitimately confess his irresoluble perplexity with much of what we have been saying, on the grounds that he finds any explanation in terms of 'a non-spatio-temporal (i.e. unobservable) personal being, somehow involved in but yet somehow "outside" or "beyond" the empirical world' to be an intolerably obscure and problematic one! And he is within his rights if he asks: 'How can you possibly arrive at such a notion? Could we possibly know anything at all about such a uniquely odd being? Have you any justifiable *analogy* for such an explanation? Can you point to any *comparable* events, states of affairs or occurrences in our experience which bring us to the point of having to invoke an "explanation" in such uniquely obscure terms as these? Have you given us anything like adequate justification for making such a desperately unprecedented and unique move as that involved in passing "beyond" or "outside" of the observable world to the unobservable, the unseen, and all the opaque obscurity that that involves? Anyway, just exactly what is the *logic* involved in your talk of "outside" or "beyond" (as contrasted with "inside" or "within") – I find this an impossibly obscure and meaningless notion indeed.' Such protests as these sum up, we suggest, what may be the greatest difficulty which our cartographer has yet faced.

VI.15 How is the difficulty to be faced? If our sorely beset cartographer surveys the writings of philosophers and philosophical theologians he will find a clue which might provide him with considerable help in surmounting this difficulty. This clue, while strikingly modern in emphasis and relevance, is for all that an extremely ancient one. He will certainly encounter it, as we shall see presently, in the works of modern post-analytic religious thinkers; yet he might have stumbled across it in reading the Stoic philosophers. For have not the classical Western religious thinkers, ancient and modern, spoken of God as 'the Soul of the World and the Mind of the Universe'?[42] The clue, that is to say, consists of the fact that the only conceivable *analogy* which would enable the cartographer to speak intelligibly and significantly of God (as described above) is a certain type of human discourse or explanation referring to the human soul or self as some unobservable, non-spatio-temporal, enduring principle or entity, 'involved in' the world certainly, yet somehow (and mysteriously) referrable to as 'beyond' or 'outside' what is empirically perceptible. We turn now to an exploration of this clue.

VI.16 A consistent and thoroughgoing empiricism has always found talk of 'selves' or 'souls' very troublesome. We noted above how a radical empiricist like Hume, faced with the traditional Western philosophical problem of the self, came to the conclusion that our knowledge of selves was strictly limited to that of *perceptions*, and argued strongly for utter agnosticism with regard to the 'substance' which integrated these, or in

which they may be said to inhere (II.10). The Wittgenstein of
the *Tractatus*, also, insisted that the mind-body problem is one
for the scientist, not for the (metaphysical) philosopher (II.15).
And Ayer also had to deny us the possibility of knowledge of
human selves as some kind of 'imperceptibles', insisting that our
knowledge of others was actual or possible sense-experiences,
giving rise to logical constructions (II.19). Our discussion so far
may have, hopefully, generated some doubt about empiricism
as an epistemological theory adequate to the totality of our
experience. Such doubt, if generated, ought now to be extended
to empiricistic discussions of the area of personal being. For is it
not clear that empiricistic scepticism about the self has been the
result of illegitimately forcing upon a hugely significant area of
our experience an epistemological strait-jacket – namely, an
epistemological account formulated specifically for the areas of
the natural and human sciences? We turn, therefore, to an
account of the self which abandons the restrictions of narrow,
rigid empiricism.

VI.17   One significant implication of abandoning these restrictions is that the starting-point for the discussion of the self
becomes the *contemplation of one's own inner experience of what is
involved in thinking and living*, rather than the detached observation of the spatio-temporal behaviour of other bodies. The
point being made here is that if this is done, the point may be
reached where we are enabled to comprehend more fully the
theist's talk of God. It may he helpful at this point if we set down
several brief quotations from I. M. Crombie, taken from a paper
already referred to. Crombie attempts to occupy 'the standpoint of the agent who is directly aware of himself', to be
distinguished from that 'of the observer, who can see our
muscles twitch, observe our brain-pulsations in an encephalo-
graph', and so on.[43] Speaking from the former standpoint,
Crombie writes:

> We are not, nor is any part of ourselves, beings outside space and time, or
> spirits, but part of our experience of ourselves is only describable with the
> aid of concepts of a non-physical kind. What we should derive from this is

not the grandiose view that we are spirits, but the ability to conceive the notion of a being independent of space, that is, a being whose activity is not at all to be thought of in terms of colliding with this, or exercising a gravitational pull on that.

Or, from the same context, we might consider this:

> ... our limited and imperfect spirituality ... leads us to think of beings who are perfectly what we are imperfectly; not that we can properly conceive of such beings, but that we are forced to frame the abstract notion of them, by the feeling that the smattering of spirit which we find in ourselves must be a pointer to the pool from which it comes.

And finally, it is worth reflecting on this:

> Our willingness to entertain the notion of a being outside space and time (of what I shall call a 'spirit') is perhaps most fundamentally based on our inability to accept with complete contentment the idea that we are ourselves normal spatio-temporal objects.

It is important to note that Crombie is not committing himself to any kind of Platonic or Cartesian dualism which holds that man is the fortuitous coming together of two different principles, soul and body, and that therefore human activities must be understood strictly in dualistic terms. Nevertheless, there is a certain irreducible *duality* attaching to our understanding and explanation of ourselves.

VI.18 Crombie's meaning is not difficult to grasp here. From the *observer's* standpoint, which we may share, we are indeed describable in terms of *physical* concepts: in terms of height, weight, age, aptitude, blood-pressure, and so on. From the standpoint of *introspection*, from that of the agent directly aware of his own thinking and behaviour, such concepts seem not merely inept but downright inappropriate and wrong. For how could we measure the length and thickness of a thought? Could we speak of the texture and weight of a memory? Is it sensible to talk of an insight being located *n* inches from our right ear, or of a conviction occupying a *space* at the base rather than at the crown of our skull? If all such are out of the question, we are forced to the conclusion that it is impossible to think and talk of mental activities in spatial categories at all, and that we must therefore formulate a quite different and more appropriate set of categories. J. R. Lucas has put it in this way: 'The doctrine that the soul is a substance in part means only this: that persons can be the subjects of a discourse in which there are predicated of them attributes and qualities which cannot properly be predicated of things.'[44] Crombie's point is that these categories and this discourse must be applicable only to *spiritual* beings (or to the spiritual *parts* or *aspects* of physico-spiritual beings). And a further important point is that the vocabulary, the categories and the discourse so generated is such that *in toto* it significantly assists in framing a notion (however negative, inadequate, and obscure) of a being who is 'perfectly what we are imperfectly'; that is, who is *quite* independent of space and time and who cannot *at all* be described or discoursed about in the terms applicable to normal spatio-temporal objects.

VI.19 As a matter of fact, the kind of philosophical discussion we have been describing here has in part been generated by the publication and discussion of Professor Gilbert Ryle's *The Concept of Mind*. The significance of Ryle's book is that he wittily caricatured the grotesqueness of some forms of traditional dualism, and persuasively drew our attention to the *extent* to which, in understanding human thinking, choosing, deciding and projecting, we rely upon observable, spatio-temporal human behaviour and speech as our guide. In doing so, he has indulged in a *reductive* analysis of discourse referring to souls or selves. Ryle has in consequence been accused of *logical behaviourism*, and, whether or no this has been proved, it is a fact that his views have evoked a considerable philosophical literature criticizing the thesis of *The Concept of Mind* and setting forth views of the self in a radically different direction from that taken by Ryle. Although this corpus of literature is pertinent to the argument being developed here, there is no room for a thorough examination of it here, but references to some significant materials may be found in the notes.[46]

VI.20 Our discussion at this point may conceivably cast light on several key-terms which we have used in a metaphysical context, namely 'inside' as contrasted with 'outside' or beyond'. We note Crombie's understandable unwillingness to describe human beings as 'spirits' and his denial that we or any part of ourselves are beings 'outside space and time'. But does this mean that human beings are therefore to be *straightforwardly* described as located totally *inside* the spatio-temporal world? Apparently not. For they cannot fully be described in terms of categories applicable to objects in space and time. We are therefore in a quandary. It will not do to say of human beings that they are *straightforwardly* either *inside* or *outside* the spatio-temporal world. We find ourselves forced, however reluctantly, to say, obscurely, that they are somehow *both*: that although they are indeed *involved in* the spatio-temporal world, they are also, and very mysteriously, *outside it*. Or, we might say, that human beings *transcend* (in what way, we know not) the empirical world. The logic involved in such uses of 'inside' and 'outside' is the only logic which casts light upon and makes intelligible the use of such words within the context of a metaphysical explanation of the world as a whole in terms of an ultimate non-spatio-temporal being (VI.13).

VI.21 Not dissimilar insights may be derived from the more severely linguistic work of Ian T. Ramsey.[47] Ramsey's conviction is 'that a true estimate of personality and a true estimate of religion stand or fall together'.[48] In practice, this means that if we wish to use theistic language meaningfully we must 'model "God" on "I".'[49] Much of Ramsey's prolegomena to philosophical theology is taken up with how the word 'I' is used in sentences. Clearly, in many cases the word 'I' is used when 'he' would have been equally appropriate. The phrase 'I did it' may on occasions mean that the act in question was done by 'me', this empirically perceptible person occupying a certain spatio-temporal location. But on other, and much more significant, occasions, the word means much more than this. On such occasions (dubbed by Ramsey 'disclosure' situations) the word is used so as to indicate 'more than' publicly observable behaviour.[50] In a series of witty stories Ramsey attempts to evoke what is involved when a person 'comes to himself', comes to an awareness of himself as more than an observable. This means, negatively, that purely objective and descriptive language is inadequate to deal with truly personal being. And since each personal being is involved simultaneously in a plurality of 'logically diverse areas', the word 'I' becomes an integrator of these. In other words, the word 'I' becomes the metaphysical integrator-symbol which serves as our model for using the word 'God'. For, in Ramsey's view, the word 'God' (like other metaphysical words such as 'Duty') arises within the context of a spatio-temporal situation which involves more than observables, an involvement the awareness of which involves a 'disclosure'. Just as, in the last analysis, we are dependent for knowledge of other personal beings on their revealing 'themselves' in and through the observable, we are likewise dependent for knowledge of God upon his disclosing himself in and through the spatio-temporal, a texture which cannot adequately be dealt with or explained in terms of observables alone and which forces us to use metaphysical words.

VI.22 Speaking of the construction of a metaphysical theology Ramsey asserts that this means, broadly, 'that we shall speak about God by qualifying any and all descriptive language – whether of people, human behaviour, or the universe – in such a way that it tells a more than descriptive story, in such a way that it evokes a disclosure. . . .'[51] Now this comes very close indeed to the programme which we pursued in chapter V (V.3 – V.22). There we delineated and described five significant areas of experience, concerning people, human behaviour and the universe, in order to bring out the sense of 'contingency' which each evokes in us, in the sense that through each is 'disclosed' the presence and activity of a non-spatio-temporal ultimate being, a disclosure which is articulated in theistic explanation and discourse.

VI.23 Again, we find not dissimilar insight and arguments in a paper by Father (now Bishop) C. B. Daly.[52] Daly quarrels with much recent British philosophy in so far as this, through rigid allegiance to the principles of thoroughgoing empiricism, has been dogmatically anti-metaphysical in an *a priori* way. Daly bases his attack on the defence of two basic metaphysical concepts, 'being' and the 'self', although here we must be concerned with the latter of these. He takes to task, for instance, A. J. Ayer, prominent amongst those empiricists who have tried to place the self beyond all possible knowledge. The mistake made by Ayer in attacking, for example, Descartes, is exactly the same made by Hume in arguing for scepticism with regard to knowledge of the self. For empiricists *assume* that existential propositions, if valid, must refer, in the last analysis, to perceptible things and objects.[53] This is why Hume insists that 'when I enter into myself, I . . . never can *observe* anything but the perception'. Hence his conclusion that 'they are the successive perceptions only that constitute the mind'. In a parallel way, Ayer interpreted Descartes' *cogito, ergo sum* as meaning in the last analysis 'there is a thought now', and from this last proposition it cannot be inferred that 'I exist'.[54] But, Daly insists, if the epistemological strait-jacket is discarded, a significantly different interpretation of Descartes becomes possible. This is that the *experience* which generated the *cogito, ergo sum* is that of 'I thinking' or 'I doubting', of an 'I' *involved in* doubting, understanding, affirming, willing, refusing, imagining and perceiving. In looking, therefore, for the self as a thing or object which could be *perceived*, empiricists have concealed from themselves and others the 'I co-existing with and involved in every experience'.[55] Or, to put this in another way, 'I know that I exist precisely in my knowing. . . .' This links up firmly with our earlier emphasis on 'one's own inner experience of what is involved in thinking and living' as the starting-point for the discussion of the self (VI.17).

VI.24 'The contemporary effort to restore metaphysics', writes Daly, 'is essentially a struggle to prevent man himself from being depersonalized by the methods of impersonal investigation and anonymous verification he has devised for science'.[56] The basic error of those empiricists sceptical of knowledge of the self is in imagining that 'the self lies *beyond* knowledge'.[57] Rather, the self 'is *in* knowledge'. The failure to reach awareness of the self is rooted in the failure to realize that 'the self is knowing, not a thing known', and that the self 'is experiencing, not a datum of experience'. Another error generated by empiricistic epistemology is that of imagining that 'all knowledge must be clear, distinct, final, leaving its solved problems behind like milestones in its march to ever new discoveries'. This is to overlook that some knowing (for example, metaphysical) has an 'open texture', or that a claim to such knowledge does not involve the claim to know about everything. Metaphysics indeed begins with the recognition of *mystery* in being and in experience, a mystery which it tries to render intelligible until that point is reached where the mystery has ceased to be and cannot become absurdity. 'The true alternative', writes Daly, 'is not mystery *or* clarity, but mystery *or* absurdity.'[58] Of course empiricists are right when they try to link up existential propositions with what can be experienced. And no metaphysician, when talking about the *metempirical* (being, the self, God), may avoid effecting 'empirical linkage' (Daly) or 'empirical anchorage' (Ramsey). But in so far as he is forced to talk of the metempirical, he cannot limit the application of terms such as 'existence' and 'reality' to empirical objects. 'My self exists, knowing exists, and they are, although involved in all spatio-temporal experience, yet certainly not contained within the limits of our talk about spatio-temporal objects.'[59] That means that 'it is impossible to deny the term existence to that without which spatio-temporal objects could not be known to exist'. Therefore, he writes, 'the metempirical is real. We know it. We are it.'[60] *Knowledge of* the self is involved even in our confession that we are failing to describe or understand it. For example, 'It is to know something about it when we say that it is not an object or a body, not-material, not-empirical, nor empirically limited.'[61] But such negative knowledge is 'a perpetual invitation to deeper reflection; but also an awareness that reflection will never come to an end of what there is to know'. Daly therefore summarizes the task of metaphysics in this way: 'to resist all pretences to explain man in terms of the non-human; to strive for ever deeper realization of the human; but to know that there is always more to know about man than can be known, that is the task of metaphysics.'[62] It follows that it is mistaken to think of a metaphysical account of the soul as some kind of 'solution' to a 'problem'. Rather, the language of the metaphysician should be construed negatively as indicating his unwillingness to accept the adequacy of the language of formal logic or empirical science in giving an account of man's reality, of 'man's self-awareness and self-discovery and self-fulfilment' (cf. VI.20). Therefore metaphysical terms such as 'mind', 'soul' and 'spirit' are not final cut-and-dried 'solutions' which put an end to puzzlement and enquiry, but '"open" ideas of inexhaustible fertility'.

VI.25 Daly echoes much of what we have been already arguing, of metaphysics as a form of existential map-making, when he discusses what is involved in testing the truth of metaphysical statements and systems. He rejects the correspondence theory of truth as inadequate to deal with the whole of human experience.[63] This theory, which holds to 'the correspondence of a statement with observational or ostensive data, or with empirical objects', fails because even the totality of such statements completely leaves out of account, for example, the personal selves of those who know and who formulate the statements. Having rejected the correspondence theory as inadequate for metaphysical constructions, he proposes that 'their truth is their adequacy to reality as a whole, or to the totality of experience'. This means that the metaphysician must allow fully in his 'descriptions and explanations for all that there is in human experience' (here he comes close to what Ramsey has called 'empirical fit'). 'Adequacy', as used here, has two senses, one negative and the other positive. Metaphysical descriptions are 'adequate', firstly, in so far as they refute the notion that merely empirical descriptions can deal with the whole of experience. They are 'adequate', secondly, when they recognize 'the existence of the metempirical within experience' and accept 'the duty of making sense of it'.[64] In so far as he does this, the metaphysician is rejecting the view that what is involved in experience is 'the infra-rational, the irrational or the absurd'. This might appear as the concession of a minimal amount of intelligibility which does not perhaps amount to very much. Yet Daly holds that this kind of concession is necessary if only to clear away the ghastly and culpable misunderstanding that the metaphysician claims completely to explain the entire universe and its contents (!) or that in positing the existence of God the metaphysical theist thereby claims to have solved every conceivable unanswered problem.[65] To the contrary, complains Daly, it is not metaphysicians but scientists and positivists (such as Bertrand Russell) who have claimed to explain (away) everything, from morality to the mind-body problem! In contrast to claims such as these, the metaphysical theist's are more modest: he tries to show, minimally, that there is an irreducible mystery in the world, and that enough rough sense can be made of this to demonstrate that being is neither self-contradictory nor absurd. Hence, in Daly's view, the classical proofs of God's existence are (although their form may conceal this) a *reductio ad absurdum et contradictorium* of God's non-existence: that is, they try to show that the ignoring or overlooking of mystery leads to the non-admission of God, hence to a mis-description which may father absurdity. To return to the discussion of the self: Daly concurs with Ramsey's views on 'the logical relatedness of "I" and "God".'[66] He remarks interestingly that there is a tendency for those philosophies which have pronounced the notion of the self to be a mistaken one to be atheistic ones. 'It would seem,' he writes, 'that to exclude discussion of the self from philosophy is to exclude discussion of God from philosophy too." The logical relatedness of 'I' and 'God' 'receives striking negative corroboration in modern positivism, for which both God and self are meaningless'.

VI.26   The discussions of the self which we have been following (VI.15f.) should bring home to us one way in which much recent philosophy has been theologically relevant: this is that those types of philosophical endeavour which stress heavily the significance of the self, of personal being, have many valuable insights to offer philosophical theism. This applies, for instance, to philosophies of personal being like that of Martin Buber, and to certain types of philosophical existentialism. But it is probable that there is one type of philosophy which might prove of exceptional value to the theist who wishes to demonstrate the similarity between the logic of God and the logic of the self, namely Continental and North American philosophical *phenomenology*. A mere word or two might indicate something of the theological relevance of this.

VI.27 That aspect of the teaching of the phenomenological tradition most immediately relevant to our present considerations is the familiar distinction drawn between the *two egos of experience*. Phenomenologists not uncommonly label these the *empirical* (or *psychological*) ego and the *transcendental* ego. One point insisted upon by many phenomenologists is that too often British empiricists, when engaging in discussions of the self, have concentrated their attention almost totally upon that self which is concerned with, engaged and interlocked with empirical *cogitata*. Hence they (the classical case is that of Hume) have too frequently spoken of the self in terms of perceptions, observations and the like, in terms of links between the self and the spatio-temporal world. The extreme position that can be reached here is the definition of the self *exclusively* in terms of perceptions and sense-data (Hume and the Ayer of *Language, Truth and Logic*). This procedure may, however, be criticized as being purely arbitrary, on the grounds that another, broader and more fruitful procedure may be employed. This is to consider the self not merely in terms of its entanglements with the empirical world but also in isolation from these. To do so is to embark on a *phenomenological analysis* of the self, an analysis which confirms and corroborates much of what we have been saying in preceding paragraphs. It is instructive to consider briefly a little of the content of such analysis.[67] Such analysis yields, for example, the conviction that the transcendental ego, since it is the ultimate core of consciousness, cannot in any sense be perceived as an object; it can never be a *cogitatum*, since it is the irreducible subjective *cogitans*. The transcendental ego is experienced whenever experience takes place, since it is itself the condition of having any experience whatsoever. This ego may by analysis be isolated from merely bodily or psychological states. The transcendental ego may indeed observe and describe that ego interlocked with the world, the empirical ego which is the subject of psycho-physical states. Phenomenologists willingly admit that it is extremely hard to find significant language in which to communicate their analysis. Indeed, they would not necessarily object to Sartre's description, the *Nothing*, if it is kept in mind that this refers to the ego considered in isolation from and denuded of all empirical contents.

VI.28   There is one aspect of the phenomenologists' teaching on the self which links up with some observations of C. B. Daly noted above (VI.24). Daly remarks that to know what the self is *not* (*not* a body, *not*-material) is to know something about it. Phenomenologists also have not infrequently appealed to *theologia negativa* for corroborative insights. Negative theology holds that a conception of God can be evoked by contemplation of what God is *not*. Similarly, since the self is not approachable as an object, a certain awareness of it can be evoked by contemplating attributes which are *not* predicable of it, and those epistemological conditions which are *not* applicable to knowledge of it. Once such contemplation has been carried out and a certain awareness generated, certain things can be said of the transcendental ego. It can be posited, for example, as the *explanation* of the paradoxical tension between *change* and *identity* in human beings. For while humans are on the one hand conscious of changes and growth in knowledge, awareness, insight, conviction and the rest, they are nevertheless simultaneously conscious of a certain *identity* and *continuity*. It is commonly held that the latter belong to the transcendental ego while the former attach to the empirical ego. It is therefore apt to describe the transcendental ego as in some sense *abiding, enduring* or *permanent* in the midst of flux and change, attributes which suggest its *timelessness.* Another insight not infrequently suggested by phenomenological analysis of the self is that while the transcendental ego may easily conceive of the non-existence of the empirical ego (considered in terms of perceptions, sense-contents, psycho-physical states, etc.), it not uncommonly finds it quite impossible to conceive of its own non-existence, an insight which probably found its first technical formulation in the proofs of the immortality of the soul in Plato's *Phaedo*. Again, phenomenological analysis of the self has resulted in the conviction (VI.18) that the categories of *space* and *time*, since they belong intrinsically to the *cogitata* of experience, are not applicable to the transcendental ego, which is in no sense an experienced *object*, and which is therefore not subject to the limitations of experienced objects. Much stress is often placed on the *freedom* enjoyed by the transcendental ego (as contrasted with the *determinations* suffered by the empirical ego), a freedom of observation, knowledge and commitment. Again, it is occasionally suggested that the *a priori* contents or structures of mind without which we could have no experience at all (and which become apparent only in and through experience) belong to and indicate the existence of the abiding transcendental ego. It is interesting that phenomenologists frequently appeal to mystical religious exercises and experiences for corroboration of the results of their analysis. For when the mystic achieves his goal of a 'contentless consciousness', a 'pure look', inner freedom from the spatio-temporal world and its determinations, he has reached that experience of 'pure subjectivity' which is identical with the experience of what phenomenologists call the transcendental ego.

VI.29 Hopefully, enough has been said to indicate in briefest outline the fruitful theological relevance of current phenomenological analyses of the self. Such analysis, if viable, corroborates and confirms that conception for which we have been arguing (VI.15f.). For such analyses yield the conception (admittedly, in many respects, imprecise and eluding the concepts of ordinary language) of the human self as some transcendent, non-empirical, abiding (permanent), non-spatial (boundless), non-temporal (timeless), free entity, known largely through negation and subjective introspection. And if our metaphysical cartographer can reasonably defend a conception of this kind, he is enabled to respond to the demand of the sceptical empiricist outlined above (VI.14). For such a sceptic complained of the unintelligibility of the metaphysical theist's conception of God, on the grounds that he could not conceive of a 'non-spatial and non-temporal (i.e. non-empirical) personal being, somehow involved in but yet somehow outside of or beyond the empirical world'. He complained, that is to say, of the apparent lack of any analogy for such a conception in human experience. The ability adequately to respond to such a challenge and to bring forward such an analogy, we suggest, depends entirely on the cartographer's ability to expound and make convincing a reasoned account of the self such as the one outlined above. John Wisdom has summarized the matter neatly:

> It is clear . . . that in order to grasp fully the logic of belief in divine minds we need to examine the logic of belief in animal and human minds. . . . The question of the reasonableness of belief in divine minds then becomes a matter of whether there are facts in nature which support claims about divine minds in the same way facts in nature support our claims about human minds.[68]

VI.30 The argument may, perhaps, be pushed one stage further. Can our metaphysical cartographer extricate himself from *solipsism* with regard to the conception he has reached of his own self? Granted that he may regard his own inner awareness of himself as incorrigible, can he reasonably move from this to the belief that his environment is constituted largely by the existence of 'other minds'?

VI.31 The problem of our knowledge of other minds is an immense one in modern philosophy, and only a little can be said about it here. The analysis of the awareness of the self given here is such that it is clear that the problem cannot be tackled (in the first instance) in terms of the *observation* of others; for the self (even one's own) lies beyond perception; it is the *cogitans*, not the *cogitatum.* It follows that the possibility of our gaining knowledge of other selves must depend on their *communicating* their awareness of themselves to us. In other words, it depends upon 'self-revelation' or 'self-disclosure'.

VI.32 The classical philosophical idealists (e.g. Plato or St Augustine) approached the question of the self (not in terms of perceptions) but by attempting to elicit or evoke such an awareness in others. They did so by inviting us to reflect upon what is involved in making mathematical, aesthetic or ethical judgments, and by arguing that such reflection must lead us to see that human minds share a certain intersubjective structure and that they 'participate in' a certain corpus of truth not derivable from experience. The perennial truth in this approach is that we may come to know our own selves by listening to the experience of others and by looking in those directions in which they claim such awareness is to be found. Awareness of the self may be generated communally.

VI.33 One theologian who has argued persuasively that our knowledge of others depends upon their revealing themselves to us is the late George F. Woods.[69] Woods's thesis is that 'Our explanation of other people is immensely assisted by their readiness to make themselves plain to us. They reveal themselves. Our knowledge of other people is mostly by revelation.'[70] In gaining knowledge of others 'something is suddenly made known to us which we could not have made known by our own efforts'.[71] A personal being 'knows himself as himself and can make himself known to others'.[72] Personal revelation 'is a mutual activity' which involves two people; the act of revelation is possible 'because they share personal being'. The act is grounded in 'community of being'.[73] Acts of personal revelation are historically conditioned, and this may generate difficulties for interpreting the records of such acts. Individuals revealing themselves 'use the thought forms and explanatory systems which are commonly accepted at the time', including 'the cosmology of the day'. Personal explanation possesses a 'progressive character'.[74] Nevertheless, 'even the most satisfying act of self-revelation is other than the person who makes it'. The self-revealer 'remains more than what he has said and done'; 'he transcends the means which he uses to make himself known and the expressions which he has used'.[75] Genuine self-revelation 'is not final in the sense that the revealer is wholly known in the revelation which he has chosen to give'.[76] Rather, the finality of personal revelation consists not in 'the revealing words and deeds but in the stability of personality which was shown in the typical acts' (cf. VI.24).[77]

VI.34 We have already examined Ian Ramsey's analysis of the way in which personal beings come to use the word 'I' of themselves (VI.21f.). Ramsey has described the use of 'I' by the significant phrase 'solipsism as the primitive metaphysics'.[78] He has rejected the view that that awareness which generates in us the use of 'I' is 'something utterly and wholly subjective'.[79] This is because 'I become aware of myself as I become aware of an environment transcending observables'. Ramsey points out that whereas we all pass through a primitive stage where we talk of ourselves in terms of third-person proper names, at a more advanced stage we come to talk of ourselves in terms of 'I'. We do so, in Ramsey's view, 'because we recognize it as being used as an indicator word by others for themselves, relating to their public behaviour and more, and we recognize that we ourselves want to talk precisely of that . . . and so of "I".' 'It is not likely,' Ramsey argues, 'that we should use "I" for ourselves, if there were nothing else but ourselves.' Since, therefore, we become aware of ourselves as we become aware of an environment transcending observables, 'the use of the word "I" commits us . . . to pluralism of persons'.

VI.35 The phenomenological analysts have come, through a different route, to much the same kind of conclusion. Phenomenologists, Koestenbaum has reminded us, have combated solipsism by insisting upon (in Husserl's words) 'the intersubjectivity of the Transcendental Ego'.[80] 'The Transcendental Ego,' he writes, 'is given as a *social reality*; it is made real by an *encounter*, by an I-Thou confrontation.' Exploration of and discourse about the transcendental ego would be hopeless apart from 'the notion of community'.

VI.36 In a significant passage, Wisdom has argued that the way in which we come to know God (whom he has named 'the Soul of the World', the 'Mind of the Universe'), might be compared with the way one knows the soul or mind of another creature.[81] Wisdom's position is that our knowledge of others depends upon a mutual interplay between observations and self-knowledge. He rejects the behaviouristic view that our talk of the consciousness of another is but 'a way of speaking of those sequences of bodily events which are the manifestations of consciousness'. This is dangerous precisely because 'it neglects the fact that though one who has never tasted what is bitter or sweet and has never felt pain may know very well the behaviour characteristics of, for instance, pain, he yet cannot know pain nor even that another is in pain – not in the way he could had he himself felt pain. It is from looking round him that a man knows of the pain, of the love and of the hate in the world, but it is also from his own heart.'

VI.37 It is, we argue, along lines such as these (VI.31f.) that our metaphysical cartographer may attempt to extricate himself from the trap of solipsism (VI.30). He can thus commit himself to the not unreasonable belief that his environment is very largely constituted by the existence of a plurality of personal selves, empirically imperceptible indeed, yet able to perform acts of personal revelation, abiding, involved in indeed yet transcending the spatio-temporal world. His belief, if reasonable, carries with it (at least) two implications of major importance. This first concerns the fact that the belief will involve him in formulating accounts and explanations of what goes on around him in the world in terms of unobservables, in terms of the thoughts, decisions and actions of personal beings described in outline above (VI.29). This means that the belief in question strengthens and broadens his response to the demand of the philosophical sceptic for some analogy which would enable him to grasp the conception of God as a metempirical personal being, immanent in, yet transcendent over, spatio-temporal reality (VI.14, 29). The short answer of our cartographer to the sceptic is that, in the light of his reasoned belief not only in God but also in personal selves, he must regard the attempt to discuss or explain the spatio-temporal world in terms of *observables alone* as one which is doomed to failure. In the light of this, the second implication should be so clear as hardly to require being spelled out: it is that his reasoned beliefs involve him in rejecting empiricism as an epistemological theory adequate to the totality (or even the greater part) or experience (VI.25).

VI.38   So far our cartographer has been constructing arguments in the light of actual or potential criticisms emanating from empiricistic quarters. But, if he is wise, he will remember that different criticisms, emanating from the side of committed religious believers, will also have to be met and dealt with. It is very probable that these criticisms will tend (as they have tended in the past) to cluster around one central one: that, no matter how laudable are the motives of the metaphysical theologian, and no matter how impressive the arguments he constructs, what he talks about in the last analysis is simply not that Being who is worshipped, trusted and affirmed in living religious faith. It follows that the arguments of such a theologian must be, at best, extremely misleading for the unconvinced, and, consequently, very embarrassing for the genuine religious believer. Hence the plea is not infrequently made that genuine religious piety should abandon all attempts at natural theology and should firmly dissociate itself from all such attempts which it finds being put into practice.

VI.39   It is this kind of objection which lies behind the not infrequent complaint that the God of the natural theologians is nothing other, in the last analysis, than a kind of 'cosmic glue' which has little in common with the object of sincere *religious* belief and practice, the 'living God' of the Bible and of Judaic-Christian worship. More serious formulations of the objection

are not hard to find. For example, John Hick, while discussing
the attempt to approach the question of God in terms of a
Wisdomian aspectual apprehension of the world, points out that
the atheist may complain to the theist that 'knowing God', in
this context, 'consists in regarding the world in a certain way, a
way characteristically different from that in which one regards
it who does not "know God".'[82] But the difference involved
would be 'purely subjective' in the sense that for the non-theist
there is 'no extra Person, whom we call God, in addition to the
world'. It may well be that the theist's view of the world is
'richer' than that of the non-theist, or more existentially relevant (or something of the kind), but to move from the theist's
perspective of the world to 'an actually existing transcendent
divine Being' is, for the atheist, 'to invoke an *ontological myth*'.
Alternatively, the atheist might describe the word 'God' (as used
by the theist in this context), as a 'logical construction' or a
'personified formula' which is valuable for appreciating the
world in a certain way. And the religious believer might, we
argue, protest that the object of truly religious worship and piety
is something altogether other than an 'ontological myth', a
'logical construction' or a Ramseyan 'integrator symbol'. The
same line of argument can be derived from a different source.
For example, Professor W. H. Walsh, in the context of a discussion of 'Metaphysics and the Supersensible', mentions the possibility of a defender of a transcendent metaphysical system who,
under pressure, concedes that his ontological assertions 'cannot
be taken literally'; and that they 'must be interpreted in an
indirect way'.[83] Walsh continues: 'To say that God exists would
amount in this view to saying that we should adopt a certain
attitude to experience: the force of the seemingly existential
assertion will come out in the consequences of accepting it, and
God will be treated *not as an actual existent but rather as a theoretical
construct*. And if the religious believer protests that this makes
nonsense of the whole concept, the answer will be that we are
concerned here with "God" as a term in metaphysics, not with
the God of religion'.[84] Once more, the religious believer will
vehemently protest that to describe the object of his life-long

devotion as a 'theoretical construct' rather than as, minimally, an 'actual existent', is to describe him blasphemously. And he will object, further, that the answer confirms his view of the misleading and irrelevant nature of the metaphysical conception of God when metaphysics is allowed to infect religion. Hence the complaints of the irrelevance, indeed the perniciousness, of natural theology.

VI.40 How can our cartographer reasonably respond to the challenge from the side of sincere and committed religious belief (VI.38)? We suggest, in various ways. For one thing, by distinguishing between certain levels. There is, for instance, the distinction to be drawn between, on the one hand, the level of *actual, concrete experience,* and, on the other, that of *reflection upon and the structuring of experience into a unified whole.* At the former of these, the cartographer is clearly appealing to an actual, concrete experience of the transcendent: he claims, for example, that in certain kinds of moral experience in certain circumstances a concrete encounter with the transcendent, with the Holy, is both possible and actual. He would likewise claim that at the level of true religion in general an *immediate* awareness of the Numinous is incorrigibly given. He might, as we saw, make similar claims in the areas of human existence, of history and of nature (V). His claim, in short, is that in innumerable areas of experience the transcendent is inescapably present and active. He claims, briefly, that man *actually encounters* God in the world.[85] But, at the second level, the cartographer is inevitably involved in reflection upon and in shaping his experience into an organic unity. And it is at *this level* that what he is talking about inevitably and necessarily appears to the outsider as a 'construction' or a 'symbol', language which appears (quite unreasonably) to be inappropriate (or offensive) to certain of the religiously committed. The question now is that of the difference and relation between the two levels.

VI.41 The fundamental difference is that argument, discourse and terminology at the second of the two levels is by necessity shaped and determined *in response to significant logical and epis-*

temological challenges. Interesting references to this are to be found in Ian Crombie.[86] Crombie points out that when the philosophical theologian tries *to fix the reference-range of theological statements* (an acceptable description of the perennial task of the natural theologian), he tries to do so '*for the critic*, that is for the man who says that he cannot see what religious people are talking about, and does not believe that there is anything which can be talked about in such a way'. On the other hand, the reference-range of theistic statements *for religious believers* is different: for them, says Crombie, ' "God" is the name of the Being who is worthy to be adored', a statement notoriously meaningless for the sceptic who complains that he does not know the object which such talk of adoration refers to. In response to this kind of complaint (however phrased and in whatever era it is made) the speculative theologian tries to offer 'a neutral account of what "God" stands for, one which does not employ any notions whose understanding presupposes a religious outlook'. In other words, in Crombie's view, the philosophical theologian does not, *quâ* philosophical theologian, try 'to describe what the Christian takes God to be', but tries to answer a logical challenge 'to the effect that theological statements cannot be meaningful because they employ a proper name which seems to be such that it is logically impossible to indicate to an inquirer what it stands for'.[87] But more can surely be said of this level of theological elucidation than this. For the religious believer, like all men, is a multidimensional being. He does not live exclusively in the sphere of supernatural revelation, but also in the spheres of morals, nature, and history, grappling with the perennial problems of human existence. And this multi-dimensionality inescapably involves him in responding to logical and epistemological challenges: particularly, by relating the insights derived from revelation to those inherent in his moral awareness, in his experience of nature, in his involvement in the realm of human existence, in his status as a historical being. And it is most difficult to see how it could do so without the aid of 'theoretical linking concepts' of one kind or another, constructs which would integrate the insights derived from those several dimensions within which all human creatures inescapably exist.

VI.42   At any rate, it may be dangerous for the metaphysical theologian to pay overmuch attention to objections emanating from certain types of committed religious believers. This is so for two reasons. The first is that objections to natural theology from the side of 'living religious commitment and belief' may be rooted in *a concealed fideism*. The trouble with the position dubbed 'sincere religious commitment' may be that it fails to take with appropriate seriousness those logical and epistemological challenges brought to bear upon religious belief and practice by philosophy and science from the Enlightenment to the present day (II). For the fideist clings to the notion that the Being worshipped and discoursed about within religious commitment may only legitimately be discussed from *inside*, but never from *outside*, the sphere of commitment itself. But consideration of this notion seems to bring us back full circle to those anti-fideistic considerations elaborated in I.21f. The second reason is that the theological ideas articulated exclusively within the circle of 'living religious commitment and belief' may not infrequently be one-sidedly and misleadingly inadequate. Such notions not infrequently include, for instance, a conception of God as 'the transcendent source of grace who brings us from inauthentic to authentic existence' (Bultmann *et al.*). Or religious believers might insist upon a notion of God as 'the eternal *Thou* of the divine-human encounter, who can only be met and addressed, never sought out by thought and expressed' (Buber *et al.*). Again, believers might emphasize God as 'the Being most worthy to be adored', or as 'that Being whom we set our heart upon' (Luther). Now no speculative theologian would quarrel with the validity of these theistic conceptions. But he would surely quarrel with the claim that they are exclusively adequate for expressing the fullness of meaning inherent in the term 'God', and that they adequately and exhaustively unpack all that Judaic-Christian theism intends (and has always intended) by the term.

VI.43 He would quarrel with the claim to adequacy on the ground that the contemporary attempt to limit theistic meanings to the area of private encounter, commitment, belief and decision is, from a certain point of view, tantamount to a disastrous retreat on the part of religious belief into a ghetto, within which it is sealed off and protected from the chilly and sometimes bleak winds of scepticism, toughmindedness, and, it must be added, intellectual openness and honesty. For, he would add, the conceptions of God apt to be cherished within the confines of religious commitment and belief are themselves one-sidedly inadequate. When the term 'God' is fully and thoroughly unpacked, vital meanings are discerned which might be overlooked if the unpacking were carried out only in the light of the immediate needs of individual piety and commitment. For by the term 'God' Hebrew-Christian belief intends not merely a 'transcendent source of grace', but also that being who integrates all finite things – the being in whom all things inhere. It intends not merely the divine pole of the religious I-Thou encounter, but also that being who is the Prime Unmoved Mover of all that moves and lives, the First Uncaused Cause of all finite existents. For Hebrew-Christian belief God is indeed 'the Being most worthy to be adored, whom we set our hearts upon', but that Being worthy of adoration because he is the Being of beings, the Lord of lords, the Being by whose will alone all things cohere. For such theism, God is indeed the 'being whom we set our heart and trust upon', but he is that precisely because he is the transcendent and creative ground of the finite world and all that it contains. It is therefore mistaken to distinguish too sharply between the so-called 'religious' and the so-called 'metaphysical' attributes of God, and hence between revealed and natural theology, especially if the distinction is drawn in order to underline the significance of the former at the expense of the latter. The truth of the matter is that trust, commitment and worship (in the fullest sense) can only be evoked by and directed towards a Being understood as possessing those attributes predicated of him by metaphysical theism. Genuine trust, commitment and worship could not be elicited by and directed towards a Being who was simply a part of the finite world, one of the beings of the universe, less than ultimate, restricted in scope, determined by anything 'more absolute' than himself. It is one of the tasks of metaphysical theology to elucidate and clarify this crucial aspect of belief in and discourse about God.

VI.44 What could we claim to have established by the substance of this little work? Hopefully, enough has been said to demonstrate that developments in recent philosophy and theology have not restricted the choice of possibilities open to theologians to that of 'syllogism or fideism'. Hopefully, we have shown that between the extremes of 'syllogism' on one side and 'fideism' on the other there is a fruitful range of possibilities open to those whose main concern is the epistemology of religion, possibilities not unworthy of the title 'rational'. It has been our intention to exhibit here what would be involved in exploring one of these possibilities.

NOTES

1. *Soundings*, Cambridge, 1962, p. 18.
2. *Theology and the Future*, p. 58.
3. *Op. cit.*, pp. 58–9.
4. *Ibid.*, p. 59 (italics mine).
5. *Ibid.* (italics mine).
6. *Ibid.*, p. 60.
7. 'The Possibility of Theological Statements', in *Faith and Logic*, ed. Basil Mitchell, London, 1957, pp. 31–83.
8. *Op. cit.*, p. 56.
9. *Ibid.*, p. 66.
10. *Ibid.*, pp. 66–7.
11. In Crombie's view, '. . . the arguments of the natural theologians . . . reveal the intellectual pressures which lead people to talk of God', *ibid.*, p. 56.
12. *Religion and Empiricism*, The Aquinas Lecture, 1967, Marquette University Press, Milwaukee, 1967.
13. *Op. cit.*, p. 43.
14. *Ibid.*, p. 44.
15. *Ibid.*, p. 47.
16. *Ibid.*, pp. 47–8.
17. *Ibid.*, p. 48.

18. *Ibid.*, p. 50.

19. *Ibid.*, p. 51.

20. *Ibid.*, p. 52.

21. *Ibid.*

22. *Ibid.*, p. 53.

23. *Ibid.*, p. 54.

24. *Ibid.*, p. 58.

25. *Ibid.*, p. 60.

26. *Ibid.*

27. *Ibid.*, pp. 60–1.

28. *Ibid.*, p. 65.

29. With VI.5–VI.8 cf. Smith's *Experience and God*, New York, 1968.

30. See, in particular, 'On the Possibility and Purpose of a Metaphysical Theology', in *Prospect for Metaphysics*.

31. *Prospect for Metaphysics*, p. 154.

32. *Ibid.*, pp. 154f.

33. *Ibid.*, p. 159.

34. *Ibid.*, p. 160.

35. *Ibid.*, p. 161.

36. *Ibid.*, pp. 160–1.

37. *Ibid.*, pp. 162–3.

38. *Ibid.*, p. 171.

39. *Ibid.*, p. 172.

40. *Ibid.*, pp. 172–3.

41. *Ibid.*, p. 173.

42. John Wisdom, *Logic and Language* I, p. 189; *Paradox and Discovery*, p. 15.

43. *Faith and Logic*, p. 57.

44. *Op. cit.*, pp. 134–5.

45. London, 1949.

46. See, for example, J. R. Lucas, 'The Soul', *Faith and Logic*, pp. 132–48; H. D. Lewis, 'Mind and Body. Some Observations on Mr Strawson's Views', *Clarity Is Not Enough*, ed. H. D. Lewis, London, 1963, pp. 381–400, and 'The Soul', *Philosophy of Religion*, pp. 273–88; C. A. Campbell, 'Ryle on the Intellect', *Clarity Is Not Enough*, pp. 278–310; A. C. Ewing, 'Professor Ryle's Attack on Dualism', *Clarity Is Not Enough*, pp. 311–38; Peter Geach, 'What do we think with?', *God and the Soul*, London, 1969, pp. 30–41. Geach's paper is important for its attempt to establish that the soul is independent of time.

47. See, for example, the essay already referred to in *Prospect for Metaphysics*; also *Religious Language*, London, 1957 and New York, 1963, chapter I; *Freedom and Immortality*, London, 1960.

48. *Prospect for Metaphysics*, pp. 174–5.

49. *Ibid.*, p. 173.

50. *Ibid.*, p. 167.

51. *Ibid.*, p. 173.

52. 'Metaphysics and the Limits of Language', *Prospect for Metaphysics*, pp. 178–205.

53. *Op. cit.*, p. 184.
54. *Language, Truth and Logic*, pp. 46–7.
55. *Prospect for Metaphysics*, p. 184.
56. *Ibid.*, p. 191.
57. *Ibid.*, p. 195.
59. *Ibid.*, p. 204.
59. *Ibid.*, p. 196.
60. *Ibid.*, p. 198.
61. *Ibid.*, p. 199.
62. *Ibid.*, p. 200.
63. *Ibid.*, pp. 201–2.
64. *Ibid.*, p. 203.
65. *Ibid.*, p. 204.
66. *Ibid.*, p. 185.
67. What follows is indebted mainly to Peter Koestenbaum's 'Religion in the Tradition of Phenomenology', pp. 174–214 of *Religion in Philosophical and Cultural Perspective*, ed. by J. C. Feaver and W. Horosz, Princeton, 1967.
68. From 'Gods', *Logic and Language*, p. 189.
69. *Theological Explanation*, chapter IX, 'Explanation by the Personal'.
70. *Op. cit.*, p. 87.
71. *Ibid.*, p. 88.
72. *Ibid.*, p. 89.
73. *Ibid.*
74. *Ibid.*, p. 90.
75. *Ibid.*, p. 91.
76. *Ibid.*, p. 93.
77. *Ibid.*, pp. 93–4.
78. *Prospect for Metaphysics*, p. 167.
79. *Op. cit.*, p. 168.
80. *Religion in Philosophical and Cultural Perspective*, p. 191.
81. *Paradox and Discovery*, p. 15.
82. See *Faith and Knowledge*, pp. 144f.
83. *Metaphysics*, p. 186.
84. *Ibid.*, italics mine.
85. 'For the theist, the word "God" does not designate a logical construction, nor is it simply a poetic term for the world as a whole; it refers to the unique transcendent personal Creator of the universe. And the awareness of God which the theist claims is not any kind of inference from the character of the world, but an awareness of God as acting towards him through the circumstances and events of his life', J. Hick, *Faith and Knowledge*, p. 146.
86. *Faith and Logic*, pp. 66–7.
87. *Ibid.*, p. 67.

INDEX